HYPNOTHERAPY SCRIPTS

A Neo-Ericksonian Approach
to Persuasive Healing

HYPNOTHERAPY SCRIPTS

*A Neo-Ericksonian Approach
to Persuasive Healing*

Ronald A. Havens, Ph.D.
and
Catherine Walters, M.A., M.S.W.

BRUNNER/MAZEL, *Publishers* • NEW YORK
A member of the Taylor & Francis Group

Library of Congress Cataloging-in-Publication Data

Havens, Ronald A.

    Hypnotherapy scripts : a neo-Ericksonian approach to persuasive
healing / Ronald A. Havens and Catherine Walters.
    p.   cm.
    Includes bibliographical references.
    ISBN 0-87630-547-8
    1. Hypnotism—Therapeutic use.   2. Erickson, Milton H.—Influence.
I. Walters, Catherine R.   II. Title.
   [DNLM: 1. Erickson, Milton H.   2. Hypnosis—methods.   WM 415
H386h]
RC497.H37   1989
615.8'512—dc20
DNLM/DLC
for Library of Congress   89-17356
                  CIP

Published by
Brunner/Mazel
A member of the Taylor & Francis Group
47 Runway Road, Suite G
Levittown, PA 19057-4700
1-800-821-8312

Manufactured in the United States of America

10

This is dedicated to
the ones we love

CONTENTS

PREFACE

This book offers simple and straightforward instructions on how to do hypnotherapy. We maintain that hypnotic trance is a common everyday phenomenon which every student or professional can and should learn to utilize in a therapeutic manner. Anyone who has ever lulled a child to sleep with a bedtime story or used an analogy to convey a new idea already has engaged in virtually the same procedures we employ during hypnotherapy. It is not a strange or exceedingly difficult process.

Our goal is to strip from hypnosis the shroud of secrecy and confusion which you may have encountered already in your efforts to learn more about it. Some authors tell you that there is no such thing as hypnosis while others claim that hypnotherapy is so powerful and complicated that it requires years of study. Some professionals warn that trance is a dangerous foray into the realm of malevolent subconscious forces while others suggest that it is only a matter of good role-playing. What is the dedicated practitioner to think or to do?

Our Neo-Ericksonian approach to hypnotherapy is derived directly from the work of Milton H. Erickson, M.D., a man who is widely recognized as the foremost hypnotherapist of the century. Erickson described hypnosis as a valuable therapeutic tool for enhancing a client's self-awareness and facilitating therapeutic communications. He used it to persuade his clients to assume responsibility for healing themselves and to give them the skills they needed to do so. Because Erickson was a consummate therapist as well as a master hypnotist, he was able to use this tool in ways that would be difficult to describe, much less duplicate. On the other hand, the basic tool itself is relatively simple and learning how to use it to create useful therapeutic interventions is not a difficult task.

In the following pages we describe this tool called hypnotherapy and discuss what it can and cannot do. We also present specific guidelines for using it in different situations for different purposes. To be more specific, we begin with an overview of the assumptions underlying our approach. Next we provide a summary of the concepts and procedures involved in a typical hypnotherapy session. The remainder of the book consists exclusively of a series of scripts designed to guide your learning about hypnotherapeutic interventions in a step-by-step manner. We offer verbatim examples of trance inductions, of metaphorical and direct suggestions for various types of presenting problems, and of trance termination procedures. To accompany this book, an audiocassette tape recording was developed to help you learn how to experience trance and to speak in a trance-inducing manner. Combine the book and the audiocassette and you have the basis for effective hypnotherapy.*

At first you may feel as constricted by our instructions and scripts as an artist working on a paint-by-numbers painting. Eventually, however, you will begin to develop an appreciation for the structure and potentials of this approach and will venture far beyond the guidelines we have provided. At that point you will have become a hypnotherapist.

Hypnotherapy can be an exciting and worthwhile adjunct to any therapeutic practice. Furthermore, when conducted in the Ericksonian manner presented here, it can provide clients with a comfortable opportunity to explore and build upon their own unconscious resources. It is not intrusive, it is not authoritarian, and it is not a power trip for the hypnotherapist. It is your chance to give a gift to your clients— the gift of peaceful inner awareness and the ability to relax deeply enough to recognize and use resources that might otherwise be overlooked or misused.

When we began this project, our intention was to produce a conceptual framework and a set of guidelines that would make hypnotherapy an accessible and useful tool for counselors and therapists whose backgrounds, clientele, and professional affiliations were as diverse as our own. We felt that if we could produce a truly collaborative integration of our own varied interests and hypnotherapeutic approaches, then perhaps the end product would have

---

*For more information about the accompanying audiocassette, contact Brunner/ Mazel Publishers (212-924-3344), 19 Union Square West, New York, NY 10003.

the broadest possible appeal and utility. Thus, although Catherine was exclusively responsible for constructing the material on habit patterns and Ron developed the chapter on pain management, every other word in the remainder of this book is the product of long hours of discussion, revision, and debate. We leave it to you to determine whether this process accomplished our purpose. Your comments, questions, or suggestions will be more than welcome and greatly appreciated.

ACKNOWLEDGMENTS

The authors would like to take this opportunity to express their sincere appreciation to all of those who have helped bring this project to fruition. First and foremost we must acknowledge Milton H. Erickson, M.D., whose writings, teachings and examples continue to inspire. There are certain words and phrases he used which seem to be so embedded in our style that they emerge here and there throughout our scripts as an unconscious tribute to his verbal persuasiveness.

The participants in our hypnotherapy workshops around the country deserve special mention, not only for their enthusiasm and dedication, but also for pointing out the need for a book such as this and encouraging us to do it. Our clients also deserve our thanks. Over the years they have been our best teachers.

Many thanks also to Stephen Gilligan, Carol Lankton, Stephen Lankton, Ernest Rossi, Kay Thompson, and Jeffrey Zeig, for generously sharing with us what each of them learned from Dr. Erickson.

Jackie Wright put in many hours word processing the various stages of our manuscript. We thank her for the excellent job she did, for her positive comments and for her tenacity in continuing to work on the scripts, even though she kept going into a trance.

Various friends and family helped us greatly as the manuscript progressed. Many thanks to Marie Havens and Larry Shiner for their editorial improvements and ongoing support. Richard Dimond made useful suggestions and

Theresa Eytalis and Sandy Mollahan demonstrated unflagging interest and encouragement in our project.

We are grateful to Natalie Gilman, Editorial Vice President, and the other members of the Brunner/Mazel staff for their guidance and assistance. Finally, while writing this book we both were shocked and saddened by the tragic death of Ann Alhadeff, Executive Editor. Ann's enthusiastic interest nourished this book when it was still just an idea and directed its initial development. Thank you, Ann.

In addition to those we both want to thank, there are certain persons each of us is individually indebted to.

Ron gives special thanks to:

— Elizabeth M. Erickson for her graciousness and generosity and to Sherron Peters and Jeff Zeig for their warmth and support. Each of you has made Phoenix feel like a second home.

Cathy gives special thanks to:

— The summer, 1983, staff of the Milton H. Erickson Foundation who graciously allowed me to spend a month working in the Erickson Archives. Ernest Gullerud deserves credit and thanks. As my professor at the University of Illinois School of Social Work, he supported me in my research in hypnotherapy. Jill Kagle, also my professor, gave me kind words of encouragement and supported my interest in Erickson's work.

— John Miller, Director of the Counseling Center at Sangamon State University, provided a positive working space for me while I was working on this book, and Vicki Thompson was very generous with her clerical and personal support. Don Yohe offered many useful therapeutic insights.

— Tami Skaggs and Therese Johnson made me laugh a lot.

PART I

Concepts and Instructions

1

A NEO-ERICKSONIAN ORIENTATION

Our interest in writing this book stretches back to our first experiences as workshop leaders training therapists and physicians in the art of Ericksonian hypnotherapy. We carefully outlined the necessary concepts for them. We compulsively instructed participants in the hypnotherapeutic process. We taught our groups how to devise unique metaphors and anecdotes. In short, we gave them all of the basics we thought they would need to become competent hypnotherapists. Yet, when practice sessions began we were faced with something we hadn't counted on: many participants became tongue-tied and self-conscious. They simply did not know what to say and the more they struggled the less they could do. We soon discovered that our exhortations to "trust your unconscious mind" just did not do the trick. They wanted us to tell them exactly what to say and how to say it. In other words, they wanted a script.

THE EFFECTIVENESS OF SCRIPTS

Our first script was a simple induction script which we incorporated into the practice sessions of our workshops. The Simulation Induction Script in this book is a modified version of this original script. Not only did the participants express gratitude for the structure and guidance this script provided, they also seemed to acquire an effective hypnotic style much more rapidly than we had seen without it. Furthermore, by the end of the workshop, they demonstrated more confidence in their ability to do hypnotherapy and seemed more comfortable with the idea of actually trying it with their clients.

Although these early impressions were encouraging, we had no objective evidence that they were accurate. Accordingly, we decided to empirically study the impact on learner confidence of using a prepared script. The subjects for our study were 13 graduate students in psychology and related fields who volunteered to participate in a free one-day workshop and research project on hypnotherapy. The entire morning was spent providing didactic information on trance, trance induction procedures, hypnotherapy and trance termination. These lectures were followed in the afternoon by a demonstration of trance induction and arm levitation. The participants were then randomly divided into two groups for a practice session. The first group contained seven participants. They were each given a trance induction script which contained suggestions for an arm levitation (the Arm Levitation Script presented in this book) and were told to pair up and take turns reading it to each other. The other group of six participants met in a different room and they simply were told to pair up and practice an induction with the goal of obtaining an arm levitation. Using presession and postsession questionnaires with the participants, and postsession rating scales with the hypnotic subjects, we discovered not only that those participants who used the scripts felt more confident, but that their actual success with subjects (measured in terms of trance depth, arm levitation and learning) was significantly higher. In the group working without scripts, for example, only one subject experienced an arm levitation, whereas all subjects in the script group experienced one. (A more detailed account of our method and results is given in Appendix A.)

The results of this simple study confirmed our hypotheses regarding the potential value of hypnosis scripts as a means of increasing skills and self-confidence. They also supported our decision to provide scripts for every step in the hypnotherapeutic process. This book is the product of that decision.

But this book contains more than hypnotherapy scripts. It also contains the basic concepts and understandings which underlie our Neo-Ericksonian approach. Our intent is to facilitate your development as a hypnotherapist, not merely to provide scripts so that others can parrot our words. In order to use these scripts as learning tools, you need a thorough understanding of the rationale for their content and structure.

The understandings you will need in order to use the scripts presented in this book are relatively simple and straightforward. Contemporary hypnotherapy is not an arcane practice derived from complex abstractions or mystical notions. The principles and procedures we use in hypnotherapy stem from a few basic observations about people, therapy and the nature of trance itself. These observations are easy to understand, they are consistent with current research, and they can be verified by personal experience.

In Chapter 2 we will examine the nature of trance and the principles of hypnotherapy. In this chapter we will discuss seven assumptions about people and therapeutic change which form the foundation for our hypnotherapeutic strategies. By becoming comfortable with the point of view reflected in these observations, you are laying the foundation for your future trance work.

Each of the following assumptions can stand alone as a descriptive summary of a particular aspect of human functioning and therapeutic change. However, when these assumptions and their implications are considered as a whole, we find that they can be used to explain the usefulness of a variety of therapeutic techniques, including the hypnotherapy techniques we present in this book. In other words, no matter what form of therapy you now use, your approach already may implicitly recognize many of these characteristics of human functioning.

PAIN IS THE PRIMARY SYMPTOM

Orienting Assumption #1: Pain is what motivates clients to seek therapy.

The common underlying feature of virtually all problems presented by therapy clients is emotional pain and suffering. Whether the presenting complaint is anxiety, depression, problems in a relationship, feelings of inadequacy, or whatever, pain and its consequences are the client's fundamental reason for seeking help.

We began developing this understanding largely as a result of an observation offered by Dr. Erickson during a lecture he gave in San Francisco in 1965. On that occasion he said:

> Every patient that walks into your office is a patient that has some kind of a problem. I think you'd better recognize that problem, that problems of all patients—whether they are pain, anxiety, phobias, insomnia—every one of those problems is a painful thing subjectively to that patient, only you spell the pain sometimes as p-a-i-n, sometimes you spell it p-h-o-b-i-a. Now, they're equally hurtful. And therefore, you ought to recognize the common identity of all of your patients. And your problem is, first of all, to take this human being and give him some form of comfort. And one of the first things you really ought to do is to let the patient discover where he really does have that pain (Havens, 1985, p. 152).

Because of our involvement in hypnosis, clients suffering from physical pain are often referred to us. As we worked with these individuals along with our traditional therapy clients, the validity and significance of Erickson's remarks became increasingly apparent. It is psychic pain and suffering that motivates people to contact therapists and therapy consists of the alleviation of that pain.

We emphasize pain as a central feature of our clients' experience primarily because pain is an easier issue for most people to understand than are psychological abnormalities. The experiential qualities, psychological consequences and interventions required to cope with pain and suffering are relatively simple and easy to grasp in comparison to the complex theoretical systems often associated with psychiatric disorders. This is true for both clients and therapists.

Mental health professionals, for example, can be so firmly wedded to specific theoretical explanations for particular diagnostic problems that it becomes difficult for them to examine and treat these problems in an objective manner. There is a tendency to impose hypothetical constructs instead of exploring the unique sources of discomfort of each individual. If a client says he/she is depressed, the clinician may immediately begin to look for "learned helplessness" or to prescribe techniques deemed appropriate for depression. If the same client had instead complained of problems with a spouse, it is possible that the therapist would have focused instead only upon this interpersonal problem and would have missed the depression. More importantly, in both instances the therapist may have missed the painful source of all of these problems.

When all problems are defined as pain, however, it seems to be easier for most therapists to set aside their own preconceptions and to examine and treat each problem from a more unbiased and genuinely inquisitive point of view. The goal becomes one of determining the nature and source of each individual's unique discomfort, rather than trying to fit the client's peripheral symptoms or presenting complaints of this discomfort into a diagnostic category.

Pain is also easier for clients themselves to understand and examine. The negative outcomes of psychiatric labeling are well documented. Defining a problem as psychic pain or emotional discomfort avoids these adverse effects. Clients cooperate more openly in treatment and are less ambivalent about revealing their relevant thoughts and feelings when we refrain from diagnoses and frame their problems only as pain.

When problems presented to a therapist are construed as a form of pain or suffering, the concepts, goals and treatments used naturally will tend to be similar to those employed to treat chronic pain. It should come as no surprise, therefore, that the hypnotherapeutic approach presented here is applicable to both physical and psychic pain. The only difference is that the procedures used for physical pain can be much more straightforward because there is less need to avoid ambivalence, resistance, self-conscious biases, and sensitivities.

Thus, there are two reasons for tracing all problems back to an issue of pain. First, our experience suggests that pain is an accurate description of the distress, hurt, and tedium which so often fill a client's life. Second, the metaphor of pain best conveys the perspective on therapy which underlies our hypnotherapeutic approach.

OUR MULTIPLE MINDS MUST INTERACT

Orienting Assumption #2: People have a conscious mind and an unconscious mind.

If you are familiar with the work of Milton H. Erickson, you will recognize this observation as the cornerstone of his hypnotherapeutic system. In some respects it is unfortunate that he used the term "unconscious mind" because this term has been used by so many other authors and thus has many potentially misleading connotations. The "unconscious mind" referred to by Erickson is not the repressed unconscious described by Freud or the rather mystical collective unconscious of Jung. Erickson used the term "unconscious mind" to refer to all of the cognitions, perceptions, and emotions which occur outside of a person's normal range of awareness. He reserved the term "conscious mind" for the limited range of information that enters the restricted focus of attention of most people in everyday life. A corollary of his observation of this dichotomy is his recognition that people try to rely upon the limited capacities of their conscious mind for direction and support, even though their unconscious mind has more resources and a better sense of reality.

The number of activities our unconscious mind carries out for us is astounding and humbling. Whenever the situation calls for the use of an unconscious memory, ability or understanding, it seems to appear magically out of nowhere whether the conscious mind wants it to or not. We reach out and catch a tossed object without giving it a conscious thought. We scratch an itch or straighten our hair without consciously knowing it. Names, dates, concepts and insights appear in our awareness. Emotional reactions bubble up from nowhere. Without realizing it, we rely upon our unconscious to master the complex skills and to provide the many insights and tools we need to cope with everyday life. Walking, talking, driving a car, finding unique solutions to puzzles, suddenly remembering to do something important, sensing the hidden implications of another's movements, and even the ability to ignore distracting sensations and perceptions all depend upon unconscious activities.

Even this brief listing of the multitude of activities of the unconscious mind suggests that a conscious/unconscious dichotomy actually is a highly oversimplified conceptual convenience. In daily life we function simultaneously on a variety of levels of perception, cognition, and response. Each of these levels, in turn, operates like an autonomous "mini-mind." Much as we may like to think that these multiple levels of activity are all monitored and integrated into a coherent set of behaviors over which we have conscious control, this does not appear to be the case. Each individual seems to possess a collection of minds operating relatively independently rather than as a unified gestalt or as a simple conscious/unconscious duet.

Although Erickson generally spoke only in terms of the conscious and unconscious levels of awareness, he clearly recognized that the origins of human behavior are much more diverse than this duality implies. In the 1940s he wrote, "The human personality is characterized by infinite varieties and complexities of development and organization, and it is not a simple limited unitary organization" (Erickson, 1980, Vol. III, Chap. 24, p. 262). At the same time, he indicated that there was not yet sufficient evidence to specify the number or locus of these different origins of human behavior. Thus, while Erickson recognized the limitations of his description of the conscious/unconscious mind as a dichotomy, he employed it heuristically to explain a variety of aspects of human functioning. More recently, researchers have sought to determine and specify the possible loci of the diverse perceptions and behaviors which Erickson labeled the conscious and unconscious minds.

For example, specification of the multiple origins of human activity was a central theme of the book *The Ghost in the Machine* published in 1967 by Arthur Koestler. Koestler proposed that human behavior can be divided into three distinct categories, each of which can be traced to three distinct layers of the cortex: the archicortex (which mediates behavior in reptiles), the mesocortex (which is more dominant among the lower-order mammals), and the neocortex (which constitutes the higher levels of cortical development and function found in the recent mammals such as primates and homo sapiens). At the same time, Gazzaniga, Bogen and Sperry (1967) were beginning to note the different attributes of the right and left cerebral hemispheres, a dichotomy which seemed to account for much of what previously had been described as "unconscious" activity. By 1978, however, Gazzaniga had become disenchanted with this simple dichotomy and was instead suggesting that "our sense of subjective awareness arises out of our dominant hemisphere's unrelenting need to explain actions taken from any one of a multitude of mental systems that dwell within us" (Gazzaniga, 1983, p. 536).

This notion of "a multitude of mental systems" was given further articulation and respectability by Fodor (1983) in his book *The Modularity of the Mind*. Fodor differentiated the various modules or mini-minds (which exist as relatively separate cognitive processing systems within the brain) along several different dimensions. For example, he differentiated the vertically organized modules or systems, such as those described by Koestler, from the horizontal divisions described by Gazzaniga. He also specified separate modules for innate versus learned processing systems and for processing systems that are localized versus generalized in their operations. Finally, he noted that some modules are computationally autonomous, while others share their resources.

The current level of understanding in neuroscience still does not allow us to specify each of these interactive modules or mini-minds exactly. We can hypothesize, however, that such a specification would include at minimum one for each of the senses (i.e., separate visual, auditory, olfactory, gustatory, tactile, and kinesthetic processing systems), and one for each of the different types of information processing centers in the brain (i.e., verbal analytic vs. integrative). Each of these mini-minds perceives every situation a bit differently, has different learning histories, different skills, and different reactions to every event. Although there appears to be some interaction and negotiation between them, there are times when they seem to act quite independently. To complicate matters further, the perceptions, reactions and responses of each may vary from one time to another in response to variations in the overall physiological state of the person.

When you interview a client, you interact primarily with that person's conscious mind. This dominant mini-mind usually is the verbal analytic mind. It has the specialized function of providing linguistic labels, verbal differentiations, and categorizations. The conscious mind uses these various labels and categories to derive rules, values, beliefs, and desires about the way things should be or ought to be. From these concepts about how things should be, the conscious mind then constructs a frame of reference, schema or model of the world. This schema or model of the world, in turn, guides or directs awareness, understanding and behavior in ways that "should be" useful, correct and personally productive. Thus, people are able to perceive, comprehend, discuss and respond to the world only in ways that are consistent with their conscious frames of reference or schemas.

One of the typical components of the conscious mind's fictionalized view of reality is the mistaken belief that it is responsible for all thoughts and behaviors of the individual. Nothing could be further from the truth. In fact, the conscious mind itself possesses very few skills and is responsible for relatively few actions or creative insights. The unconscious aspects of the mind play a major role in the events of everyday life. Nonetheless, the verbal conscious mind usually believes that it is the only source of decisions, emotional reactions and responses of that person.

In order to maintain its delusion of self-importance, the conscious mind must account for all internal events and behaviors in ways that make them seem to be coherent or logical results of *its* activity. Thus, the conscious mind constantly takes credit for and finds explanations for the activities of the various mini-minds over which it actually has no control and about which it is unaware. After years of practice, it becomes very good at this. In fact, the conscious mind may be able to offer such impressive rationalizations and explanations that even the most skilled therapist may be taken in by them.

Accordingly, when talking to clients it is important to remind yourself that there are many thoughts, perceptions and actions occurring either outside that person's range of conscious awareness or outside that individual's range of conscious control. The multiplicity of mini-minds responsible for these events are referred to collectively by the term "unconscious mind." Because the unconscious mind typically consists of the bulk of the mini-minds within an individual, it is not surprising that it is much more observant, wise, intelligent, adaptive, and skillful than the conscious mind.

The relationship between the conscious mind and the unconscious mind is similar to the relationship between the captain of a ship and the crew. The captain (conscious mind) develops charts and maps (schema or frames of reference) and uses these charts to tell the sailors (unconscious mini-minds) where to go. The captain also decides what skills the sailors must learn in order to operate the ship. This arrangement works out reasonably well as long as the captain's charts are accurate, the crew has learned the right skills, and close contact is maintained between the captain and the crew to make sure things are going smoothly.

The conscious mind, like our captain, perceives and responds only to a translated version of the world. Unless reality is consistent with the charts, the conscious mind will tend to ignore it. For example, a person whose conscious schema contains the erroneous belief that he/she is not attractive to anyone may remain completely oblivious and unresponsive to the obvious overtures of an interested party. People ordinarily do not consciously perceive or act upon things that are not allowed by their map or cognitive schema.

Memories, internal thoughts, images, and expectations are constantly generated by the various mini-minds. Any of these may be accepted and acted upon or ignored and misinterpreted by the conscious mind. Whether some perception, memory or image gets acknowledged and included in its original form or gets distorted or shoved back into the realm of the unconscious is a function of how well it fits into the conscious mind's schema and of how flexible that conscious schema is. Things that conflict too much are rejected.

The conscious mind also may misunderstand or miss much of what occurs inside and outside the person simply because it can pay attention only to a limited number of things at a time. Thus, a person can be so absorbed by a good book that a question from a friend will go unheard or an appointment will be forgotten. Other things go unnoticed because they are so subtle, brief or remote that they are not perceived consciously. These sources of information are overlooked or ignored simply because they are too minuscule or too far away, not necessarily because they conflict with the conscious charts. Changes in pupil size of another person, for example, may not be noticed consciously, even though subsequent emotional reactions may indicate that this cue was perceived on an unconscious level. Likewise, if the conscious mind has difficulty accepting or translating certain thoughts or sensations into verbal representations, they also will go unnoticed. Thus, fleeting sensations or activity in remote areas of the brain or body often will be ignored.

The thoughts and perceptions of the *unconscious* mind are not constrained by the conscious schema or framework. Like the sailors on our ship, the unconscious mini-minds notice icebergs and other dangers whether they appear on the captain's charts or not. They also notice and produce many things the conscious mind tends to ignore or overlook. The problem faced by the conscious mind is how to maintain a conscious frame of reference or chart that is both comfortable and useful while at the same time not ignoring the skills and important new inputs from these various mini-minds. Navigational errors or even disasters may occur if the conscious captain refuses to use the sailor's skills, to accept new information, or to change the charts of reality. Not all of what these mini-minds do or report is pleasant, accurate or useful and some of it may bring the accuracy of the entire view of reality into question. The problem, therefore, is what information to let through and what to block out, what to use and what to ignore, what to encourage and what to discourage.

In actuality, it is difficult to specify accurately the exact nature of the information allowed in by the conscious from the unconscious because the boundaries between them are neither static nor clear-cut. At times the boundaries between these regions are sealed off and the uptight conscious personality is totally unaware of all unconscious understandings and activities. On other occasions this same individual may drift off into a reverie where previously unconscious learnings or ideas suddenly spring to mind. Sometimes these memories or ideas inspire, sometimes they amuse, and, at times, they startle, confuse, or even terrify the conscious mind. The things that inspire or amuse may be incorporated into the conscious charts or schema, but the things that cause torment may precipitate a panicky retreat back into the apparent safety of the conscious frame of reference. Any retreat or blocking off of the unconscious may signal the beginnings of serious psychological, emotional or adjustment difficulties.

INJURED INTERACTIONS CAUSE PAIN

Orienting Assumption #3: An injured, inadequate, or inappropriate relationship between the conscious and unconscious minds can give rise to a variety of painful emotional, behavioral and interpersonal problems or symptoms.

Although some problems are a consequence of specific biophysical malfunctions, a majority of the difficulties experienced by psychotherapy clients are the result of poor coordination between conscious and unconscious activities. Ideally, the fully functioning individual would have a relatively free flow of material between the conscious and unconscious minds and the activities of the two would be cooperatively integrated and coordinated (cf. Erickson, Rossi, & Rossi, 1976). The understandings, abilities and reactions of each mini-mind would be reviewed and evaluated to determine their overall validity and value to the functioning of the total personality and these inputs would be integrated into a coherent, adaptive coping pattern.

In this sense, each person is like a large family or an entire community populated by specialists who, if allowed to work together, would contribute to the smooth and efficient operation of the entire system. But if that group or community becomes dominated by a misinformed or biased leader (such as the conscious mind) who ignores everyone who disagrees with the official party line, the end result may be inefficiency, corruption, dissent, or a straightforward revolution. Similarly, the individual who is dominated by a misinformed conscious mind or who has an inadequate, and/or antagonistic relationship between the conscious and unconscious minds may experience unnecessary emotional turmoil, self-defeating patterns of thought, and self-destructive patterns of behavior.

There are clients, of course, whose difficulties and discomforts simply are a result of conscious misinformation or ignorance. When this is the case, counseling may consist of providing new information or correcting misinformation. Such counseling is a straightforward and rewarding process for everyone.

But it is more likely that a majority of your clients are experiencing problems because of a conflict or a lack of coordination between their conscious and unconscious minds, not merely because of misinformation. For one reason or another they are unable to operate in the smooth and efficient manner typical of cooperative conscious/unconscious functioning. The relationship between their conscious and unconscious minds has been injured and, as a result, they feel out of control and are unable to take charge of themselves or their lives.

An injured or inadequate conscious/unconscious relationship can produce as much pain as a dislocated elbow or a severed limb. Something is out of place, out of control, or not working properly. The functional integrity of the individual is damaged or threatened in some fashion. As a result, that person's ability to cope comfortably and efficiently is compromised, symptoms develop, and pain or suffering is experienced.

Some injuries are produced by external sources and some are self-imposed. Parents who forbid crying or tease children when they get their feelings hurt may impose a disconnection between conscious awareness and unconscious emotions. Loss of a loved one, physical torture, or sexual abuse also may create conscious/unconscious dissociations.

A self-imposed injury to the conscious/unconscious relationship may be intentional or it may be accidental. When some aspect of the unconscious thinks, perceives or knows something that the conscious mind cannot tolerate or accept, the conscious mind may intentionally sever all awareness of and communication with it. If, for example, one of the unconscious mini-minds notices indications that a friend is lying, the conscious mind may ignore all subsequent information from that mini-mind in its attempt to protect itself from that knowledge. The conscious mind also may accidentally lose touch with other unconscious sources of information simply because it is unaware of them or is unable to utilize them. As mentioned previously, some unconscious events (such as the recognition of pupil dilation in another person or a fleeting thought) may occur so rapidly or so subtly that they are overlooked or masked by other events.

Whether intentional, accidental or from external sources, the end product of an injured conscious/unconscious relationship is either an unwillingness or an inability to manage unconscious processes appropriately. This means that the person may 1) lose contact with potentially valuable unconscious resources and information, 2) experience an inability to heed useful unconscious warning signals, 3) misunderstand or misinterpret unconsciously produced events, or 4) inadvertently misuse powerful unconscious abilities in counterproductive ways. Any of these outcomes is painful and produces symptoms which can disable clients to the point where their lives become difficult and unpleasant. From their point of view, something just is not working right.

A few examples may help clarify how malfunctions which occur as a result of inappropriate conscious/unconscious relationships end up producing the symptoms experienced by your clients. Anxiety, for example, typically is the result of fleeting but vivid internal images of things that could happen in the future, such as heart attacks, accidents, insanity, failure, ridicule, or embarrassment. These clients have taught their unconscious to scan the future continuously in an ongoing search for anything and everything that can go wrong. Their generalized anxiety is a consequence of their constant but unrecognized exposure to vivid thoughts or images of all the most painful worst-case scenarios their creative unconscious minds can produce. In a similar fashion, panic attacks and phobias usually involve the rapid but intense experience of an unconsciously produced image or thought. They differ from general anxiety only in that these phobia-producing images typically involve a *specific* dreaded outcome.

A fear of enclosed spaces, for example, was unwittingly self-induced by one client who had the remarkable ability to experience vividly all of the sights, sounds and sensations of the walls of a building caving in on him. Whenever he entered a building, he could hear the support beams snap, see the walls crumble, and feel his body being crushed by them. Furthermore, he could create and experience this entire scenario in only a few seconds and emerge from such thoughts with amnesia for them. All he was left with was an awareness of the remaining intense startle response occurring in his body and a feeling of fear, responses that anyone would experience under similar conditions. After he became aware of the previously unconscious events that were the source of his anxiety, he was able to learn how to use these same imagery abilities in more pleasant ways.

As is the case with many clients, this man's inappropriate and self-destructive use of unconscious talents began as an appropriate, intentional coping device. Originally, while helping his father renovate old homes, he trained himself to carefully monitor things that could go wrong as they removed pillars and walls. Such monitoring eventually became an overlearned, uncontrolled unconscious response of which he was unaware.

Ignored or uncontrolled immersions in unconscious images also can be responsible for depression. Depression, however, often seems to be the result of a continuous review of every previous painful, unpleasant feeling or experience the client has ever had. A chronically depressed, suicidal young woman, for example, discovered that she reviewed and relived every personal failure or trauma in her life over and over again whenever things were not going her way. Even though she no longer meant to do this, it was obvious to her that she originally had used this self-punitive review as a way to justify her intense anger toward herself and her family. When she finally recognized that her own thoughts were responsible for her unpleasant state of mind, she rapidly began learning how to use her unconscious to construct more positive self-affirmations and expectations instead.

Many people have unconscious abilities they are not taught to be aware of or to use properly. Sometimes the resulting inadequate conscious/unconscious relationships can produce anxiety, panic or depression. Sometimes they also can produce an unwarranted fear of one's own unconscious abilities. A 25-year-old woman sought therapy because she was concerned that she was insane. The sole evidence for her concern was her discovery that she could imagine herself doing horrible things, such as killing her parents, her spouse, or herself. Her "treatment" consisted merely of instructing her to imagine herself standing on her head in the middle of the street or eating a hot dog or doing any of hundreds of other silly things. She was allowed to discover that her unconscious could and would produce any image she could think of, including murder. The simple establishment of an informed relationship with her unconscious abilities reassured her and provided her with an immensely valuable skill, the ability to visualize.

The results of a poor relationship between the conscious and unconscious minds can be a bit like the results of a poor relationship between an uninformed but haughty tour guide and a knowledgeable, skillful bus driver. The bus driver knows where all of the interesting sights are located, has information about them, and has the skills needed to get there. But the tour guide, being unwilling to admit ignorance or to ask for help, continues to issue directives to the bus driver and to make up information about places that have no significance. Eventually, the guide may force the driver to take an impossible road to nowhere, much to everyone's discomfort. Such often is the case with the conscious mind. It means well, but it takes us down paths we might be well advised to avoid.

INJURIES ELUDE EXAMINATION

Orienting Assumption #4: Clients generally are unable or unwilling to admit, examine or experience the source of their pain or may fear the perceived consequences of doing so. These attitudes make it difficult to identify or soothe the pain and may perpetuate the symptoms.

Imagine that a man limps into your office and tells you that he feels terrible. When you ask him why he feels so bad, he says he does not know. After a lengthy interview, which reveals nothing, you finally decide to have him relax, close his eyes, and report what comes to mind. He eventually reports a pain in his right leg, so you ask him to be more specific. He indicates that he feels a sharp pain in the heel of his right foot and then remembers that he first felt it when he was walking barefoot in the park. When you ask him to carefully examine his right foot, he discovers a large thorn embedded in the heel. Although he initially is sickened and revolted by the wound, which is becoming infected, you eventually manage to get him calmed down enough so that he can remove the offending thorn.

Further questioning reveals that he always tries to ignore his injuries. He hates the sight of blood and the thought of being cut terrifies him. He notes that he has had several severe infections over the years, but usually his ignored wounds have healed by themselves.

Now, imagine instead that the original discomfort stemmed from a psychological source of pain. This minor change in the scenario provides a glimpse of the problem frequently faced by the psychotherapist. Clients often do not want to know what is bothering them. In fact, they actively want to not know it.

It is hard enough for people to closely examine physical injuries and defects. We know how the human body is supposed to look and when it fails to conform to that image we react with panic or disgust. Gaping wounds, infected sores, disfigured bodies or broken bones create powerful emotional reactions, especially when they happen to us.

Even when the injury belongs to someone else, however, we tend to look away and feel the urge to run from the gruesome scene. But if the injured party is going to receive any help, someone has to examine the problem very closely. Paramedics, nurses and physicians, for example, have to learn to suppress their natural aversions and allow themselves to inspect the damage objectively, decide what can or should be done, and do it. Somehow they have to stay calm and respond to the situation competently.

The same is true when the source of pain is some unpleasant thought, perception, memory, belief, or fear which the client's conscious mind is unable or unwilling to acknowledge or examine. Before anything can be done to correct the problem, the source of the pain must be located and thoroughly inspected.

Almost invariably, therapy clients have a source of emotional pain which they have not faced directly or examined closely. It is difficult to pay attention to any unconscious event that is frightening, confusing or inconceivable. On the other hand, a decision to ignore something in the hope that it will go away may lead to unpleasant and sometimes severe consequences. Anxiety, depression, alcoholism, and psychosomatic illnesses may reflect a misplaced stoicism, an attempt to overcome pain by ignoring its presence.

This tendency to overlook or deny internal thoughts or experiences because they are distasteful to the conscious mind is perfectly understandable. We all do it to some extent and to some extent it is adaptive. However, therapists must recognize that pain, whether physical or psychic, is an important source of information about what requires therapeutic attention. It is a signal, a valuable alarm which indicates the nature and location of the problem and provides an indication of the corrective action needed. A consistent refusal to examine painful thoughts and feelings in the mistaken belief that ignoring them will eliminate them eventually results in greater pain and more severe symptoms. As pointed out by Fisch, Weakland and Segal (1982), it is the client's attempted solution to a problem that makes the problem worse. An unwillingness or an inability to pay close attention to the source of the discomfort prevents the person from doing anything to correct the problem or to alleviate the suffering.

PAIN LEADS TO THE SOURCE

Orienting Assumption #5: Pain is the best guide. It automatically draws attention toward the source of the problem. The therapist must focus on the pain and help the client do so as well.

Pain calls attention to a problem. That is what it is designed to do. If the injury or source of pain is severe, it will override all other stimuli and demand attention. Pain from less dangerous sources of discomfort may recede into the background while attention is captured by something like a fascinating movie. But as soon as the movie gets boring, even those minor aches and pains will reappear.

When someone is in pain, his/her unconscious responses will reveal the discomfort. The nature and location of physical pain is revealed by the way that person walks, adjusts his/her position, or unconsciously rubs the affected area. The source of psychological pain is revealed by a client's symptoms, by the topics the person avoids, the images that drift through his/her mind, the words used to express a thought, or the meanings imposed upon ambiguous stimuli, such as projective tests. These and many other unconscious indications of the existence and source of pain occur whether the conscious mind is aware of that pain or not.

Conscious awareness can be diverted from the experience of pain by a conscious decision to ignore it or by an intense external stimulus. But whenever attention ceases to be distracted by external events or the person relaxes and drifts inward, awareness is captured by any existing discomforts and directed straight toward the source of that discomfort. Physical pain seems to be magnified in the quiet darkness of a bedroom because there is nothing else entering awareness. Sources of psychological or emotional pain also are hardest to ignore in those quiet moments, such as the time period just prior to the onset of sleep. Thoughts keep drifting toward those unwanted, unpleasant feelings, worries or memories.

Even during sleep, pain cannot be avoided. The fitful sleep created by physical pain is mirrored by the disruptive emotion-laden dreams and daydreams of someone in psychic pain. The unconscious is relentless in its efforts to direct attention toward unresolved problems and unattended injuries. It tries to make us aware of our foolhardy ignorance of the source of our pain, whether we want it to or not. By focusing upon your client's pain, you will enable his/her unconscious to direct you straight to the source of the problem.

AWARENESS PROMOTES HEALING

Orienting Assumption #6: Once the source of pain is identified, clients will reflexively correct or eliminate that problem, if they can. People are inherently self-corrective and self-healing.

Both the conscious mind and the unconscious mind attempt to rationally protect the person and to do whatever can be done to ensure his/her comfort and survival. Given adequate information, they do an impressive job. When information is suppressed, ignored, or unavailable for inspection, however, the individual cannot develop a co-ordinated, integrated method of handling the situation.

To use a physical analogy once again, consider the case of a man recovering from a severe lower back injury. When referred for treatment, he could barely walk and was experiencing painful muscle spasms in his back and legs. He also was suicidally depressed. His strategy for dealing with his injury and pain had been to ignore them and to attempt to do things the way he had prior to his accident. His struggles to suppress his awareness of pain were exhausting him and his efforts to do things the way he used to were producing constant irritations and strains on the injured tissues.

Treatment consisted primarily of teaching him how to calmly focus his attention upon the most intense central locus of his pain. This immediately produced both conscious and unconscious changes in his behavior. As long as he paid close attention to the source of his discomfort, he was able to remind himself consciously to avoid certain activities, such as lifting heavy objects. Whenever he started to do something that was too strenuous, the focal point would become slightly more intense as a danger signal to him. Furthermore, simply by paying attention to fluctuations in the intensity of the pain in that focal area, he unconsciously began to alter his gait and other movements in ways that reduced his pain overall.

By focusing upon the signals produced by an area of discomfort, clients allow all of their conscious and unconscious resources to be brought to bear upon the problem. Instead of fighting with their discomfort or overlooking the valuable implications of that discomfort, they can learn to use it as a source of information about how to lead their lives more comfortably and responsibly. This is as true for therapy clients as it is for chronic pain patients.

When therapy clients focus upon their discomfort and discover that the source of their problems is a particular memory, image, desire, belief, behavior, or interpersonal relationship, they usually will begin to do something about it immediately if they know what to do and can do it. They may end an unpleasant relationship, alter their lifestyle, change a belief, or revise an expectation. Sometimes they will do this consciously and intentionally. On other occasions the changes occur at an unconscious level, seemingly by themselves.

Consider, for example, the case of a woman who sought help because she was becoming terrified of driving. She was unable to remember exactly when or under what circumstances she had first experienced her anxiety, but she did know that it had gotten increasingly worse over the past year. She was taught how to enter a light trance and then was asked to focus her attention upon her fear. As she allowed her experience of that fear to grow in intensity, she was asked to report her thoughts and internal images. She seemed surprised by her realization that her most intense anxiety was somehow connected to one particular place on the highway en route to work and she was unable to find any reason why this particular place should be so fear-inducing. Nonetheless, she was reassuringly told that her unconscious could find a way to cope with this problem and was aroused from the trance.

Two weeks later she reported that she was having no difficulties driving at all. When asked to account for the sudden change, she was unable to do so. She just laughed and stated that all she knew was that every day for the past two weeks she had tried to examine that place in the road that seemed to make her nervous. She was curious about why it caused such a reaction. But no matter how many times she reminded herself to look it over carefully, whenever she got to that spot something distracted her. One day it was a song on the radio, the next day a spot on her glasses, and another day a passing car she thought she recognized. Each day she drove by that place without realizing it until it was too late. A year later her phobia still had not returned and she still had not examined the view at that particular place in the road.

As this case illustrates, the unconscious can resolve a problem in a creative manner. This case also demonstrates an important hypnotherapeutic maxim: *the development of an awareness of the nature and location of the source of a discomfort is not the same as providing a theoretical explanation for why that source exists.* From our perspective, it is not necessary to explain why a problem exists in order to change it. The operative concept in our approach is *what* rather than *why*. Even though some clients will be able to remember when or why they developed their problems or symptoms, they typically are no longer experiencing them for the same reasons. Frequently, they are not experiencing them for any reason at all. They are just old, outmoded, counterproductive habits which once served a purpose but no longer do so. Furthermore, people are so exquisitely complex that any effort to specify the exact cause of a poor conscious/unconscious relationship usually results only in oversimplified speculations and rationalizations. Different people experience similar problems for different reasons and many different events typically contribute to the development of any given problem. Finally, an explanation for why the problem developed can be relatively useless. Explaining why an injury occurred does not facilitate its treatment. The important issue is where the injury is and what it looks like, not why it happened.

It also must be emphasized at this point that many therapy clients, and especially therapy clients referred for hypnotherapy, may actually be suffering the effects of an undiagnosed biophysical problem rather than an unexplained psychological problem. Olness and Libbey (1987) found that roughly one out of every five hypnotherapy clients had an underlying physiological basis for their presenting problems. For these people it is critically important to differentiate a physiological source of suffering from a psychological one. Obviously, efforts to impose a psychological explanation could be very detrimental to their well-being. Fortunately, most of these clients seem to know at some level of awareness that their symptoms are biologically based. As a result, when asked to focus their attention upon their pains and deficits and to follow them to their origin, these individuals often can pinpoint the physiological basis for their problems.

This phenomenon is exemplified by the case of a man who was referred with a diagnosis of paranoid schizophrenia. Over the course of the previous three years he had undergone a marked change in personality, had become delusional, and had experienced visual hallucinations. When asked to focus upon his symptoms while in a light trance state, this man reported that it felt as if his head had been blasted with electricity. He then related this feeling to an incident wherein he was struck by lightning. Although this event had occurred only days before the onset of his early symptoms, neither the client nor any of his physicians or therapists had postulated a causal relationship. A neuropsychological evaluation revealed considerable residual organic impairment consistent with a massive electrical discharge over the surface of the cortex. His presenting symptoms of suspicion, grandiosity, confusion, and emotionality abated once he had obtained a realistic description of the source of his problems. After rehabilitation training provided him with alternative coping strategies, he returned to his family and to a productive life.

There are numerous other examples of similar incidents in our files. When encouraged to allow their pain and discomforts to direct their attention to the source of their symptoms, clients have been able to locate physical symptoms which have led to the discovery of previously undiagnosed brain tumors and cysts, viral infections, hormone imbalances, allergies, kidney infections, and cardiovascular problems which were the actual cause of their difficulties.

The primary goal and purpose of therapy, therefore, is to enable clients to admit, accurately locate, and precisely define the source of their pain. Clients with adequate conscious and/or unconscious problem-solving and coping skills automatically will engage in the self-healing, self-corrective actions needed. All they require is a clear view of the source of their problem and an opportunity to consider a variety of new ways of thinking or doing that will take care of that problem. The therapist does not have to do anything other than give these clients an opportunity to engage in the self-healing process.

ASSISTANCE MAY BE NEEDED

Observation #7: Not all clients can correct their problems without help. Some need to learn new skills before they can do so. It is best if this learning occurs at an unconscious level.

Mere identification of the problem creating a client's discomfort does not guarantee that the client has the conscious/unconscious resources needed to resolve that problem. Some clients require a variety of hints suggesting alternative solutions before they can figure out what to do. Others may be able to figure out what to do, but may not be able to carry out their selected solution. At times, therefore, you will need to help your clients develop the skills they need and find potential solutions to their problems.

On the other hand, it would be presumptuous and disrespectful to assume that anyone is able to determine the right solution or the required skills for another. The complexity and uniqueness of each person prevents us from knowing the best action another individual can or should take in any given situation. In fact, even the conscious mind of that person has such a limited and biased view of the situation that it may be unwise or inappropriate to leave such decisions up to it.

Hypnotherapy offers a way out of this dilemma. Trance-induced experiences can be used to convey a host of skills and problem-solving strategies to the unconscious mind. Clients can be taught to view events from different vantage points, such as a disinterested newspaper reporter, a child, or a wise sage. They can learn to alter their sensations and perceptions in a myriad of ways: amplifying some, minimizing others, and transforming a few into an entirely different experience. They can be shown how others have solved similar problems. In brief, the abilities and understandings of the various unconscious mini-minds can be introduced to each other while new abilities and understandings are added at the same time.

Given the motivation and opportunity, clients will use these added unconscious resources automatically in whatever way seems appropriate or productive to them. By helping your clients build new reservoirs of inner resources, you will enable them to solve problems in their own unique way without interference from your biases or from their own conscious prejudices and concerns. More importantly, you will enable them to learn how to trust, use and expand their own unconscious capacities in the future and, thus, how to avoid unnecessary pain and suffering.

CONCLUSION

The Neo-Ericksonian approach to hypnotherapy presented in this book is based upon the proposition that chronic emotional pain and chronic physical pain are highly comparable, if not identical, experiences. Both stem from a problem or injury. Both signal the existence of that injury and guide attention toward it. Left unchecked, both can result in a myriad of additional problems or symptoms. Both are unpleasant experiences which people are highly motivated to eliminate if at all possible. Most importantly of all, both can be treated or alleviated in a similar manner, i.e., by building and utilizing the unconscious self-healing, self-corrective resources of each client. Although other therapeutic approaches may accomplish this goal, our Neo-Ericksonian approach is specifically designed to do so.

Given the orienting assumptions presented above, we begin therapy with the attitude that our clients' pain will provide an avenue to a clear view of the problem. We also assume that this clear view will motivate clients to use their creative unconscious energies in an effort to devise an appropriate solution to the underlying problem. We recognize, however, that some people will require additional hints and encouragements before they can develop or utilize a solution and minimize their discomfort. This view of the process of hypnotherapy is the basis for the induction and suggestion strategies described in the following chapters.

2
—

ON DOING HYPNOTHERAPY

The conceptual orientation presented in the first chapter defined the general goal of our approach to therapy as the identification and elimination of the source of emotional pain. In this chapter we will provide the specific information and instructions you will need in order to use a trance state to help your clients identify and ease their pain.

First we will explain why trance is an especially valuable therapeutic tool. Then we will look at some basic rules you can use to guide your decisions about when and with whom to use trance or hypnotherapy. Next we will examine the nature and purpose of each step in both the Diagnostic Trance process and the hypnotherapeutic process. Finally, we will tell you how to proceed from here in your development as a hypnotherapist.

HOW TRANCE AND HYPNOTHERAPY WORK

The term "trance" refers to the daydreamy state of mind often experienced by people when they meditate, listen to music, attend a long lecture, drive on a freeway at night, undergo a hypnotic induction, or wait patiently in a therapist's waiting room. The only difference between these various types of trance is the mode of induction. Whether elicited by a hypnotist or induced by a long stretch of highway, a trance is a trance.

Trance is a state of *passively focused inner awareness*. This state is associated with a vivid involvement in imagined events, a shift into a context-free, literal understanding of words or phrases, and a removal of the restrictions ordinarily imposed upon unconscious abilities and responses. The hypnotherapy process is designed to take full advantage of all of these characteristics of trance.

The primary source of difficulty in therapy is that most clients are unable to pay close attention to critical issues for very long or at all. Their conscious attention typically is caught up in an actively defensive or critical analysis of one thing after another. They protectively screen their perceptions, censor their responses, and use all of their conscious effort to maintain the integrity of their current conscious framework. During trance, however, attention may be highly *focused* or restricted to one or two things for long periods of time. Furthermore, this stabilized attention can be focused *internally* upon vivid thoughts, images or sensations that ordinarily would be overlooked or denied. Finally, this internal focus of attention tends to involve a *passive observer* state of mind not unlike that experienced by the members of an audience enthralled by a symphony or enchanted by a good story. Events merely are observed, not censored or altered.

As a result of these changes in conscious attitude or state of mind, clients in a trance are able to pay closer attention to their own unconscious sources of potential information and guidance. They also are able to more comfortably accept indirect and even direct statements from the therapist which they might otherwise overlook or reject. Finally, while in a trance state, clients can experience imagined events with such clarity and relaxed involvement that they undergo many of the same changes in learning, performance and belief that they would in the actual situation.

Because of these and other characteristics, there is a natural tendency for therapeutic changes to occur spontaneously whenever a person enters into a trance. As clients relax and become more calmly aware of internal events, their attention is automatically drawn toward any sources of pain or discomfort. Those sources of pain and any thoughts, memories or images associated with them may be inspected relatively comfortably and calmly from within a trance. This inspection stimulates the natural self-healing impetus described in Chapter 1 and often leads to spontaneous changes in behavior, understanding or attitude which will alleviate the problem. Thus, effective hypnotherapy frequently can be accomplished merely by eliciting a trance and encouraging the client to use that relaxed state of mind to learn whatever his/her unconscious has to offer.

With most clients, however, it is necessary to do more than merely induce a trance state. Usually, it is necessary to gently guide attention toward the murky or disturbing areas of internal discomfort, using hypnotherapeutic techniques such as metaphorical allusions or symbolic references. Such indirect approaches or metaphorical hints provide a nudge toward an understanding of the problem and/or its solution, but still rely heavily upon the client's own initiative and resources.

Although the newfound skills, conclusions and solutions clients develop for themselves in response to such permissive or indirect approaches seem to be the most effective, a few clients require a more straightforward or direct approach. For these individuals, specific therapeutic instructions or statements are used. A trance state simply makes it more likely that these clients will accept and act on your therapeutic communications. Clients are more relaxed and receptive to new ideas or behavioral directives when in a trance.

It should be noted that hypnotherapy does not depend upon the increased suggestibility commonly associated with hypnosis. *Giving clients the hypnotic suggestion that when they awaken they will no longer feel anxious, depressed, etc. simply does not work. The notion that hypnosis magically gives the hypnotherapist the power to demand the disappearance of symptoms is a popular misconception which probably stems from faith healing and exorcism or wishful thinking! We strongly urge you to resist any temptation to try to use hypnosis in this unrealistic and unsophisticated manner.* Efforts to use hypnosis in this way not only are largely ineffective, they also create a great deal of resistance, convince clients that hypnosis cannot help them because it does not work, and perpetuate superstitious beliefs about the nature of hypnosis itself.

PRE-TRANCE CONSIDERATIONS

Here are some basic rules and recommendations for you to consider before you begin to use hypnosis in your practice.

A.   *Client Oriented Issues*

1.   We recommend that you *do not use* these hypnotherapeutic approaches with psychotics or borderline personality disorders. These individuals already have a very tenuous degree of control over their conscious experiences and the use of trance with them can add to their confusion or create anxiety and paranoid ideation. Also, the use of hypnotic techniques with borderline personalities can add to the interpersonal relationship problems frequently encountered by these people in the normal course of events.

2.   Although the hypnotherapeutic process can be used successfully with clients of below-average intelligence, the

procedures used with these individuals typically need to be more direct, concrete or straightforward than most of the approaches presented in this textbook. In general, the scripts presented in this volume require at least average intelligence and vocabulary.

3. The hypnotherapeutic procedures presented here can be used effectively with persons suffering from neurological impairment, as long as the organicity has not resulted in a loss of verbal skills or abstract reasoning abilities. Where abstract reasoning is problematic, direct suggestions and inductions should be used. When verbal skills are impaired, nonverbal approaches not covered in this text are called for.

4. When a client has an external locus of control, and thus believes that the resolution of his/her problems depends entirely upon changes in someone or something else, the initial goal of therapy is merely to precipitate a shift toward an internal locus of control. Hypnotherapy will not be effective as long as an individual believes that he/she has no control over or responsibilities for his/her own feelings, thoughts or behaviors. At first, therefore, the Diagnostic Trance procedure and various metaphors should be used to help the client begin to experience at least a minimal appreciation for the relationships between his/her thoughts, images, feelings, and behavior and develop an acceptance of personal responsibility for their occurrence.

5. Many habit problems, such as smoking, overeating, etc. are very resistant to change. Only clients who genuinely are committed to change tend to respond to any form of intervention, including hypnosis. With individuals who view hypnosis as a magic cure which will somehow *make* them cease their habit pattern, the odds are that hypnosis will not work. This failure, in turn, will confirm their conviction that they cannot change. Trance facilitates alterations of habit patterns and makes the change process easier, but it does not and cannot force it to occur. The first order of business, therefore, is to use hypnosis to motivate the person to change, not to use it to try to force such changes. While this is true for other problems as well, it is especially true for habit problems.

B.   Procedural Issues

1.   Although not absolutely necessary, it is best to conduct hypnotherapy in a quiet, comfortable atmosphere with as few distractions as possible. A comfortable recliner may facilitate the process.

2.   For most clients, especially during the first several sessions, trance is a tenuous or fragile state. They will "snap out of it" every now and then (in response to particular words, sensations, outside noises, or internal thoughts), at which point they will tend to swallow, shift their position slightly, or even open their eyes. When this happens, simply say, "That's right, you can drift down into trance and back up to the surface quite automatically and then you can drift down again without any effort at all." Then proceed with whatever you were doing previously.

3.   Whatever the patient experiences or does during the hypnotherapy process must be accepted as appropriate and potentially useful. Never imply or suggest that they have done something wrong, that they have done something unusual or weird, or that they have failed in any way. Even if they suddenly start telling you that it is not working, that nothing is happening, or that they want to stop, that is fine. Do not become disappointed or argumentative. Just inform them that they are doing fine, but that it takes some people several sessions to get comfortable with the process.

4.   Clients know more about what they need than do their therapists. If a client protests or declines a hypnotherapy session, it usually is wise to abide by his/her wishes.

5.   Don't panic! There is no way to predict or control a person's experiences while that person is in a trance. Every individual encounters something different when she/he becomes absorbed by or comes into contact with his/her own inner unconscious thoughts and feelings. At times clients will experience some very disturbing material. If someone becomes upset, simply ask what is happening and reassure him/her as the problem is explained to you.

6.   If a client falls asleep, just wake him/her up the way you would any sleeping person. Do it gently but firmly. Use a more active or direct approach with that individual during

the next session or have him/her assume a less comfortable position, such as sitting up.

7. Clients are their own best therapists. In general, the primary goal of the hypnotherapist is to evoke a trance state within the client with the assumption that the client can use that state as an opportunity to do therapy. Accordingly, we recommend a minimalist approach to hypnotherapy. Do as little as possible. Do only what is necessary to evoke a trance and then stop doing a trance induction. Do as little as possible to promote therapeutic activity during a trance and then sit with a quiet expectation of success. As a general rule, *it is always better to do too little than too much.* Begin with a simple trance induction and add more elaborate induction comments only if a trance does not develop. Once a trance develops, simply encourage therapeutic activity. If nothing happens, use general metaphorical implications. If the client still seems to be avoiding direct awareness of therapeutic issues, use more direct suggestions or statements as a last resort.

8. Clients can accomplish a lot between sessions if given the tools to do so. The final script presented in Chapter 3 is a trance induction process designed to help clients develop the ability to enter into and utilize trance on their own. We recommend that you use the procedure described in this script after one or two hypnotherapy sessions. Some clients seem to find it helpful if the therapist makes a tape recording of this session which they can use at home for added practice. Again, this approach recognizes the fact that clients are their own best source of therapeutic material and that ultimately they are responsible for their own trances and their own therapeutic change.

THE DIAGNOSTIC TRANCE PROCESS

In our training to become psychotherapists, many of us learned to rely upon two rather limited ways of understanding our clients. Most of us learned to think of people in terms of traditional diagnostic categories and/or to focus on the presenting problem as the major source of information about a client. Both diagnostic categories and problem-focused assessments provide a sort of shorthand way of sorting and using information about clients and, as such, perform useful functions. However, we have found that this shorthand way of thinking about clients often prevents a perception of the unique aspects of each problem and may block a therapist's ability to select an individualized approach for each client.

We do not believe that just because clients have similar presenting problems or can be placed into the same diagnostic categories they necessarily are experiencing the same thing for the same reason. Nor do we believe that they should be treated in the same manner. Your clients can experience similar patterns of symptoms for entirely different reasons. A simple phobia, for example, may be most accurately described as a self-induced panic reaction for one client and as a natural response to an unconsciously held misunderstanding for another.

In order to develop a clear concept of the specific source of each client's problem, therefore, we recommend that you conduct a thorough Diagnostic Trance before you begin therapy. The Diagnostic Trance involves an exploration of the various unconscious images and associations connected to the problem. The procedures involved are very simple.

1. *First of all, ask your clients to close their eyes, to relax for a while and then to concentrate upon the unpleasant sensations or feelings they associate with the presenting complaint.* When clients follow these instructions, a very light trance is usually the result. In this light trance they begin to become accustomed to the rituals of hypnotherapy (e.g., eye closure and relaxation) and they begin to learn to pay attention to internal events. More importantly, with this procedure clients recognize that they are learning how to examine and take charge of themselves. Learning to recognize and utilize the potentials of one's own previously unconscious thoughts, feelings and images is a significant part of learning to become fully aware and fully functioning.

2. *Ask your clients to wait patiently and quietly while observing those unpleasant sensations and to just report whatever thoughts or images suddenly come to mind.* The idea is to help clients observe their discomfort without thinking about it and to just allow associated memories or ideas to spring to mind. Tell your clients to report anything they experience and observe them very carefully as they do so. If you notice any changes in expression or indications of a change in their state of mind, ask them to report what is going on inside.

This simple procedure often reveals a pattern of thinking, a series of images, or even a specific memory which is connected to and responsible for the client's pain and other symptoms. The client may report a voice repeating a particular phrase, a "secret" decision to block out an unwanted bit of information, a seemingly unrelated image, or a previously forgotten incident.

The relationship of these internal, automatic or unconscious associations to the pain or problems experienced by the client may be obvious to everyone involved or their implications may be very obscure and uninterpretable at the time. When the relationship to the problem is not obvious, the resulting images still offer a useful basis for deciding which metaphors to employ during hypnotherapy. This will be discussed in more detail later.

When this procedure reveals the internal events or activities responsible for the discomfort, some clients immediately will be able to figure out how to prevent further pain. The next, and final, step in this procedure is designed to facilitate this outcome.

3. *Ask your clients to find a thought or image which removes or displaces their unpleasant feelings.* Many clients know in precise detail at an unconscious level exactly what they can do to resolve the problem. From the moment they enter your office, these clients know what will help. Many other clients have all of the resources required to figure out what they need to do. All they lack is the opportunity to do so.

Accordingly, we have incorporated an optimistically permissive expectation of self-healing throughout this book, including this opportunity for it to occur spontaneously in the initial Diagnostic Trance process. As indicated previously, we maintain a minimalist philosophy of therapy which postulates that the therapist should never do more than is necessary and should always encourage or allow the client to do most of the work. If a client enters your office with some secret understanding of how to resolve the problem or already has access to the unconscious resources necessary to do so, you might as well use them. This portion of the Diagnostic Trance, therefore, is devoted to discovering whether or not those understandings and resources already exist.

If your client discovers a particular thought or image which does eliminate the uncomfortable feeling (e.g., the fear, depression or grief), then therapeutic change can be accomplished merely by having the client practice this new skill until it becomes habitual. If your client is unable to find and use a thought or image that relieves the painful feelings, then the hypnotherapeutic procedures outlined in the following section should be employed.

Specific scripts for the Diagnostic Trance process are not provided because it is a highly individualized interaction or conversation between you and your clients about their internal experiences. The exact wording of your instructions and questions is not the critical issue. Just follow our general guidelines, be open-mindedly curious about your clients' inner world, and accept whatever they offer as potentially useful information.

Example of a Diagnostic Trance

A brief example may help clarify the flow of events in a typical Diagnostic Trance. Here is a summary of the procedure used with a 20-year-old university student who was referred for treatment because of her long-standing inability to speak in the classroom.

Therapist: Now I would like you to just close your eyes, sit back and relax for a while. That's right. Let your arms relax, your legs relax, your face relax. Just let your entire body relax as you continue to listen to me and pay attention to your own thoughts and feelings.

You have said that you feel paralyzed and upset whenever you are asked a question during a class or are expected to speak out loud. You also have indicated that you become terrified whenever such things happen to you.

Now, I know this is not a nice thing to ask, but I think it would be very useful if you could let yourself remember now that terrified feeling and tell me what you notice as you do so. In other words, I would like you to remember that feeling so clearly that you actually begin to feel it *right now*. Can you do that?

Client: Yes, I think so.

Therapist: Good, And what do you notice when you do so? What do you experience?

Client: I feel scared, really upset.

Therapist: O.K. But where do you feel that scared feeling? What part of your body feels scared? Where do you notice it most?

Client: My stomach I guess. And my throat.

Therapist: And what is it you feel in your stomach and throat?

Client: A tight feeling, kind of hot and tight.

Therapist: Good. Now, as you let that hot tightness in your stomach and throat get more and more intense, I would like you to just pay very close attention to those sensations. Pay very close attention to them without trying to think about anything else at all. Just let your mind focus on those sensations while we wait and see what your unconscious mind can tell us that might be useful. Just pay close attention to that terrible hot tightness and tell me whatever thought or image just seems to come into your mind as you do so. Whatever it is that you become aware of as you pay attention to that sensation, I want you to tell me about it. And I'll just wait until you notice something that just seems to pop into your mind out of nowhere. (*long pause*)

Client: That's funny. I just remembered Mary. She sat in back of me in eighth grade. We were best friends. I really liked her. I was talking to her when Mr. Brown screamed at me that day.

Therapist: What day was that?

The young woman went on to describe the traumatic incident which precipitated her anxiety and led to her inability to speak aloud in class. Evidently, her teacher had yelled so loudly at her for talking that he had virtually stopped her in her tracks. She felt frozen with fear and was completely unable to answer any of his questions about why she was talking and what she was talking about. This inability to speak generated more anger from her teacher and further frightened her. Although this incident eventually led to a poor adjustment to school and probably was singularly responsible for her problems with speaking in a classroom setting, she indicated that she had not thought about it in years and had no idea beforehand that it was the source of her problem.

This example of the Diagnostic Trance illustrates the simplicity and therapeutic benefit of gently directing attention toward the underlying discomfort. The client's own unconscious understandings are allowed to surface while the therapist merely waits and provides the incentive needed to focus upon what otherwise would be avoided. A Diagnostic Trance always should be conducted prior to any decision to use the hypnotherapeutic process described below.

STEPS IN THE HYPNOTHERAPEUTIC PROCESS

A hypnotherapeutic trance session consists of the following steps:

Step 1: Transition Into Trance

Step 2: Trance Induction

Step 3: Metaphorical Guidance Toward the Source and/or Solution of the Problem

Step 4: Direct Statements or Suggestions Regarding the Source and/or Solution of the Problem

Step 5: Trance Termination
   a) rehearsal and review
   b) ratification
   c) reorientation
   d) distraction

Step 6: Follow-up Evaluation

This brief summary of the flow of events in a typical hypnotherapy session is the core framework around which the scripts in this book are organized. Accordingly, the purposes and procedures involved in each step must be reviewed before you begin selecting specific scripts upon which to base your hypnotherapeutic efforts.

Step 1: Transition Into Trance

The first time a hypnotherapeutic trance is used with a client it is appropriate to initiate the transition from an ordinary conversation into trance work with a comment such as, "I would like to do something a bit different for a few minutes that I think might help. O.K.?" Or you might simply say, "Now might be a good time to begin working with hypnosis. O.K.?"

When your client agrees, you should give a behavioral directive (e.g., "Move to this chair," "Close your eyes") that you will use on *all succeeding occasions* as your transition into trance. Exactly what directive you provide will depend upon the seating arrangement in your office and upon what position you believe will be most comfortable for you and your client, but here are a few typical examples:

> "Why don't you move over to this chair. It is a recliner and you probably will be more comfortable if you can just sit back, close your eyes, and relax. That's right."

> "Just get into a comfortable position there and go ahead and close your eyes as you allow yourself to begin to relax. That's right."

> "So sit up straight with your hands resting comfortably in your lap and allow your eyes to close as you take a deep breath and feel your body relaxing more and more completely. That's right!"

Each of these instructions provides a nice transition cue *and* initiates a light trance at the same time. The authors almost invariably have their subjects close their eyes right from the beginning of the hypnosis session and then add some comments about relaxation. This immediately eliminates distracting sights in the environment and focuses your client's attention inward upon thoughts and sensations. Usually a light trance quickly develops.

Transition comments and instructions should follow the basic format used in these examples, but it is not necessary for you to say exactly the same thing each time. What is important is that you *ask your client to do the same thing each time*. This provides a clear experiential signal or cue that something different is about to happen. Once your client has experienced a trance following a specific transitional shift into a new position, whenever that client is instructed to assume the same position in the future he/she will tend to reenter trance again. This phenomenon, probably a result of simple associative learning processes, makes reentry into trance a simpler, more automatic process on succeeding occasions and eventually may even eliminate the necessity for a formal trance induction.

Step 2: Trance Induction

The purpose of any trance induction procedure is to provide instructions and stimuli that promote entry into the trance state of passively focused inner awareness. Trance is a natural event which every client has experienced many times almost every day of his/her life. Most people, however, do not know how to intentionally allow themselves to shift into this mode of functioning. Thus, it is up to the therapist to provide a situation which first elicits trance and then teaches the client how to stay in that trance while observing internal unconscious events.

In order to help your clients learn how to allow a trance state to develop, you need to be able to say the right things in the right way. The trance induction scripts presented in this book contain comments that will trigger trance states in a majority of subjects. Some of the scripts rely upon confusion to create a trance, some use boredom to stimulate a trance, and most include many puns, non sequiturs, and other wordplays to propel the person into a less normal, less conscious state of mind. When spoken with the voice tone and voice rhythm you will acquire by working with our practice tapes, these scripts can be very compelling.

We have provided several different induction scripts because different individuals and different situations call for different approaches. The Induction Selection Criteria presented at the beginning of Chapter 3 will help you decide which induction may be most useful with each of your clients.

Step 3: Metaphorical Guidance

Metaphors, anecdotes and allusions are used during hypnotherapy for the same reason that they are used in nontherapeutic settings, i.e., because they communicate ideas persuasively, provoke personal associations to the subject matter, and stimulate creative thinking. Whether used within a hypnotherapy context or not, virtually all metaphors can trigger a rich assortment of conscious and unconscious associations, any one of which may direct a person's attention toward personal issues or provide a useful insight. Thus, all of the metaphors presented in this text also could be used with some probability of beneficial effect during an ordinary conversation or a nonhypnotic therapy session.

Actually, the metaphors and anecdotes presented in this text incorporate a variety of persuasive rhetorical devices, such as allusions, similes, rhyme, poetic rhythm, etc. As a result, these metaphors and anecdotes stimulate therapeutic events in several different ways.

On the one hand, the basic content and events of the story may be symbolically *descriptive* of your client's personality, situation or problem. This descriptive analogy can lead that client toward a more direct examination and appreciation of an undesirable or counterproductive internal state of affairs than might otherwise be possible. In effect, the metaphor says to your client, "Here is what you are doing to yourself!" "Here is the situation you are in!" "Here is how you look to others!" The metaphors presented in this book are designed to do this in an indirect manner that does not threaten the conscious personality or arouse resistance to the message. The metaphor merely plants the seed of an idea at the unconscious level. If that idea is useful, it will grow to fruition over time at a conscious level and result in a conscious realization.

In addition, the events of each metaphor may be *prescriptive*. In other words, the story may contain examples of problem-solving strategies, coping skills, or new perspectives which your client could apply to his/her circumstances. It is assumed that many clients will simply recognize at some level the merits of the problem-solving approach offered in this story and will use it later as a template or guide to resolve their own problems. Other clients will experience such a vivid involvement in their own imaginary participation in the story that they learn the strategies vicariously.

The chains of association initiated by the characters, events, settings, or words used within each story offer another source of therapeutic benefit. By scattering key words, phrases, incidents, and symbols throughout each metaphor, we have enabled you to gently guide or direct thinking toward specific topics such as childhood, family, sex, anger, loss, etc. Again, your client is indirectly encouraged to consider issues that ordinarily might be ignored or avoided.

Finally, clients themselves may invent or project a therapeutic meaning onto any metaphor. Because pain continually draws attention toward the source of difficulties, when therapy clients hear an ambiguous message their inner search for meaning almost invariably leads them toward the very things they are trying hardest to avoid, i.e., pain, secrets, unpleasant memories, the need for change, etc. Clients naturally assume there is a reason why their therapist is telling them a particular story and they immediately begin searching for the hidden message or personal relevance. If the metaphor is too obviously descriptive or prescriptive, they may notice the implications right away and reject the message and/or the message bearer. Thus, the less direct or more symbolic the personal relevance of a metaphor, the more a client is forced to rely upon intuition and unconscious insight to decipher the meaning.

Our experience suggests that the *therapeutic significance and impact of self-generated meanings are inherently greater than anything we might have said directly.* Discovered meanings are always more powerful than imposed meanings and the ambiguity of metaphors makes them an ideal way to promote such discoveries.

The most ambiguous metaphors are called general purpose metaphors. These metaphors contain ideas and suggestions which are relevant to the full functioning of anyone in the general population, but they have no obvious personal relevance to any specific individual. As such, they allow each client complete freedom to "discover" a personally relevant implication or meaning for him/herself.

If a general purpose metaphor fails to elicit significant self-discoveries, however, then it may be necessary to provide a metaphorical message that is somewhat more personally descriptive or straightforwardly prescriptive for that individual. Ideally, this personalization increases the client's sense that what the therapist is saying is specifically directed toward him/her (which, in turn, may increase the motivation to discover and use the hidden meaning), but remains subtle enough to avoid creating reactance or resistance.

There are at least three possible sources of topics for personalizing metaphors. First, you may be able to use the metaphors presented by your clients themselves during a Diagnostic Trance, an ordinary therapy session, or a discussion of their dreams. When one client announced that he felt like he had been run over by a truck, metaphors dealing with driving and with animals trying to cross expressways were used during that session. Similarly, when another client reported a dream about swimming, metaphors about the ocean, fish and other related topics were incorporated into her hypnotherapy.

A second way to signal clients that you are using metaphors personally relevant to them is to select ones that reflect your own metaphorical associations to that particular individual. Focus upon the client's outstanding physical features, behavior, interpersonal style, or whatever characteristics seem to stand out in your mind. Then ask yourself what thoughts or images these features create in your own imagination. Erickson once used a story of an ironwood tree with a broken branch as a metaphor with an elderly gentleman suffering phantom limb pain from an amputated arm (Haley, 1985, pp. 324-325). We have used stories about fluttering birds, a crazed vase, and the process of making maple syrup, to name a few, because some quality of the client conjured up these associations.

The third and perhaps the primary source of metaphorical associations is the client's problem itself. This method of selection has an obvious advantage in that metaphors which are related in some symbolic manner to the presenting problem often contain inherent implications for alternative problem-solving strategies. Thus, a person whose presenting problem is that he/she is anxious and high-strung might suggest a metaphor involving a guitar player who finally learned how to play well when he/she loosened the strings on his/her guitar.

Logically, the most effective metaphors are derived from all of these sources at once. This enables each metaphor to reflect the client's view of the problem, the therapist's view of the client, and the therapist's suggested solutions to the problem. Such individualization would be expected to maximize the client's interest in and vicarious participation in the metaphor and to enhance the therapeutic impact.

It probably should be mentioned at this point that we prefer naturalistic metaphors that are based upon actual events or real phenomena rather than fictional or allegorical stories. Our experience suggests that this naturalism gives the metaphor more legitimacy and validity than a made-up tale.

This book contains scripts for general purpose metaphors that can be used with virtually anyone. It also contains scripts for problem-focused metaphors that we have found to be useful with certain types of problems and clients. We recommend that one or two of the general purpose metaphors be used following the initial trance induction. If this general approach stimulates therapeutic change, then there may be no need to use a more problem-specific metaphor. On the other hand, if neither the general purpose metaphors nor the specific reference metaphors seem to produce results, then it may be desirable to use a more direct approach.

Step 4: Direct Statements or Suggestions

While metaphors provide a gently indirect or permissive way to help clients discover more about themselves, the potential value of straightforward messages and instructions cannot be overlooked. Many clients could benefit greatly from direct statements about the source of their problems or from specific suggestions about what to do to enhance their situation if they were less defensive or resistant to change. A trance state improves the ability of clients to hear and use such direct messages without defensiveness or resistance.

Direct *statements* regarding the nature of a problem or its solution are firm expressions of the therapist's opinion about what is causing the problem or what needs to be done to resolve it. They should be used only when the therapist is reasonably certain that his/her opinion is valid and when the client has demonstrated a willingness but a seeming inability to accept these insights. The trance state may enable the client to accept these observations more comfortably and fully than he/she can in the waking state. We also frequently present these direct statements as comments a third party (another therapist, perhaps) might tell a client if given the opportunity. It seems to be harder to reject a message when the message bearer is not present.

Direct *suggestions*, on the other hand, usually involve an indication that the client subsequently will experience a change in a particular thought, feeling, behavior, or perception. The implication is that this event will happen automatically without a conscious intention. The prescribed response presumably will disrupt or replace the response which is causing the problem.

Direct hypnotic suggestions are very useful under certain circumstances. If the solution to a problem is relatively straightforward and involves the clear communication of one simple idea or behavioral assignment, then a direct approach is the most parsimonious. If a client is a highly compliant hypnotic subject, then direct suggestions may be effective. Finally, as a result of the influence of television and movie portrayals of hypnotherapy, many clients seem to expect that direct suggestions will be a part of the process. When this is the case, it makes sense to use them, if for no other reason than to satisfy that expectation.

There is a problem with the use of direct suggestions. Because they are so blatant, the likelihood of conscious resistance is very great. Unless the suggestion is acceptable to the person on a conscious level or the person is so responsive to hypnotic suggestions that the conscious mind is unable to prevent unconscious compliance, they will not work. For this reason, we prefer to surround direct suggestions with distracting metaphors or to embed them within an anecdote. This minimizes the possibility of conscious recognition and resistance and maximizes the probability of an unconscious response.

It should be obvious that direct suggestions can work only when the client is able to respond. Vague prescriptions such as "You will no longer experience your symptoms!" rarely work because clients do not know consciously or unconsciously how to accomplish that outcome. They must be told what to do.

In addition, we usually include reassuring reasons why it is possible and appropriate to eliminate or replace the undesirable responses. The idea is to motivate the client to comply with the suggested alteration or response for some reason other than merely because you say so. Thus, the client should be informed that the symptoms can or may now fade a) because they no longer are needed, b) because they are based upon an erroneous idea, c) because the client now knows how to avoid creating them in the first place, or d) because there are better ways to accomplish the same purpose. When followed by an indication of what the client can think or do instead, this approach often promotes rapid resolution of the problem.

The combined use of direct suggestions and direct statements is demonstrated in the following case. An 18-year-old college student was referred for treatment of panic attacks which had not been reduced by relaxation training, desensitization or psychotherapy. The Diagnostic Trance exploration revealed that his attacks were triggered by any event which seemed to provide evidence consistent with his secret fear that his overuse of marijuana for several months had done irreparable and major damage to his brain. He knew consciously that this belief probably was unwarranted, but he remained terrified that it might be true. A light trance was induced and he was told in no uncertain terms that he no longer needed to experience panic attacks because he was not brain damaged, because all of the things he thought might indicate brain damage were more easily explained by other things, and because he was not adequately trained to make such diagnoses in any event. He was then told that whenever he began to think he was brain damaged he would hear the therapist's voice telling him this was not true. These admonitions were repeated several times with professional conviction and he was aroused from the trance. He immediately expressed feelings of relief and since that time he has not experienced a single recurrence of his symptoms.

It should be noted that this client responded to direct requests for change because the changes requested were appropriate and acceptable to him. Had the suggested changes been inappropriate, contrary to his ethical or moral principles, or potentially dangerous, it is unlikely that he would have complied. In fact, inappropriate or untenable suggestions may result in animosity on the client's part. Just because a client is in a trance and thus is more amenable to suggestions and new ideas does not mean that he/she has become a mindless automaton. People in a trance may become more willing to accept and act upon ideas that are desirable or helpful, but also they seem to become *less* willing to respond to ideas that are inappropriate or intrusive.

Step 5: Trance Termination

The trance termination process is a multipurpose closing ceremony. *First,* the person is allowed to review what was learned and to rehearse any newfound skills and any changes in attitude or behavior that may be useful to him/her in the future. *Next,* an opportunity is provided to experience something that will validate or ratify the trance as an unusual and potentially important event. *Finally,* as the client arouses from the trance to an externally focused waking state, distracting comments are made to prevent conscious analysis, rationalizations or dismissal of the previous trance experiences.

This stage of the hypnotherapy process obviously involves a crucial series of events. Complex as it may seem, however, each of these aspects of the trance termination process is relatively easy to accomplish and can be conducted in much the same manner with every client. As a result, only one trance termination script is provided in this book. Variety or individualization is not particularly necessary or useful during this final termination stage.

For example, the portion of the trance termination script which is designed to promote the review and rehearsal of new learnings is purposefully vague and nonspecific. This enables clients to integrate whatever they learned, even though it may not be what the therapist thought was being taught. Clients learn what they need, not necessarily what we offer to them. Allowance must be made for their inventiveness and creativity. Thus, the review and rehearsal segment offers clients the opportunity to solidify their unique learnings.

Trance ratification is accomplished most simply by offering suggestions for amnesia about the trance events and for a distortion of the sense of the amount of time spent in a trance. Both amnesia and time distortion are rather typical consequences of the trance experience anyway, perhaps because the contrast between the relaxed trance state and the ordinary waking state is so great that it precipitates state-dependent learning and memory (cf. Rossi, 1986). This effect is magnified by the insertion of distracting or irrelevant comments about some previous topic of conversation or some item in the room immediately following a return to wakeful awareness. Not only do these distracting comments inhibit a critical analysis of the trance process, they also minimize the transfer of trance memories into conscious awareness and promote the experience of amnesia. By taking advantage of these natural consequences, the therapist can easily demonstrate the unusual nature of the trance experience to the client.

Arousal from a trance also is easily accomplished. A noticeable shift in voice tone and speed into a more conversational style immediately signals the end of the trance process. A waking state orientation is further established by redirecting awareness back toward external stimuli, such as sounds from outside the room, a ticking clock, a source of light, etc. An indication that the unconscious mind can allow conscious awareness to return to a normal, comfortable and refreshed feeling reassures the person that the transition into wakefulness will be smooth and automatic. Finally, an expectant pause, a shift in position and a deep breath by the therapist all imply that this part of the session is over.

People do not get stuck in a trance, though they may be reluctant to leave such a relaxed state and will take their time doing so. Some clients may require a rather direct command to "Wake up *now!*" but that is rare and such a directive should be used only as a last resort. Many therapeutic understandings can develop during this transition stage and it is wise to allow clients to take their own time to go through it. In general, we recommend that therapists begin to terminate a trance process at least 10 minutes before the desired end of a session. This allows enough time for a transition into wakefulness, a period of reorientation, and either feedback from the client or a general conversation about therapeutic issues.

Step 6: Follow-up Evaluation

Feedback from the client can be obtained after one or two irrelevant or distracting post-trance conversations have occurred. This gives your client a chance to forget those things that are best forgotten and to put some distance between the trance and an analysis or review of it.

Feedback at this point usually will be spotty or minimal, but most people will be able to remember particular things they enjoyed, things that increased their involvement in the process, or things that disrupted the trance (e.g., outside noises or a particular topic). For feedback regarding the therapeutic benefits of the hypnotherapy process, however, you probably will have to be content to wait, watch and listen. Your client may immediately demonstrate some insights, changes in attitude, alterations in emotional reactivity, or changes in behavior, but usually such changes are not obvious to the client, are not obviously related to the trance, or do not manifest themselves until later. Only the passage of time will allow an accurate determination of therapeutic benefit and change.

Clients may or may not attribute whatever changes occur over the course of the next few days or weeks to their hypnotherapeutic experiences. If they do, such attributions may be gracefully acknowledged with an indication that you merely provided the opportunity for them to do whatever was in their own best interests. If they do not see a relationship, however, no effort should be made to point out to them how their changes are related to specific comments or suggestions you gave them during the hypnosis session.

The changes precipitated by hypnotherapy often seem fortuitous, naturalistic or spontaneous because they typically emerge from and are controlled by the unconscious mind. Clients should be allowed to take credit for them and to attribute them to their own unconscious resources. This acceptance of personal responsibility for desirable changes enhances self-esteem, promotes expectations of continued success in the future, and gives people a profound respect for and willingness to rely more fully upon their own unconscious storehouse of understandings and abilities. After all, their welfare is the primary concern, not the perceived power or skill of the therapist. Accordingly, we suggest that you give credit where credit is due—to the client and to the various components of the client's own unconscious mind.

GUIDELINES FOR THE USE OF THIS BOOK

Now that you are familiar with the background concepts, format, rationale, and rules of hypnotherapy, we recommend that you do the following:

1. If you have not already listened to the audiotape accompanying this text and participated in the trance process, now is the time to do so. Take your time learning how to allow yourself to enter into a trance. This experience will give you more information more directly about the nature of trance than any discussion or description of it we could offer. Listen to both sides to determine which is the most effective for you.

2. After you have experienced a trance (even a brief or a light trance will do), find and begin reading aloud the transcript of that induction. [The transcript for Side A begins on page 52 and the transcript for Side B begins on page 59.] At first, try to simulate the voice tone and rhythm of the demonstration. We do not suggest this because we believe that either of these demonstrations is perfect or contains the exact voice tone, rhythm or style that every hypnotherapist should use. We suggest it because we want you to learn how to speak from within a trance and we have found that the easiest way to teach someone how to do this is to have them imitate a session that already is associated with their own entry into trance.

    We want you to learn how to speak from within a trance because you must learn how to speak in a manner that is consistent or harmonious with the trance state of mind. When you speak from within a trance, you guarantee that your voice rhythm, tone, volume, and pacing as you read the trance scripts are appropriate for the experience of trance. What you say during hypnotherapy is important, but *how* you say it is equally important. Our scripts will help you learn what to say, but you also must learn how to say it in a manner that is conducive to trance. The easiest way to accomplish this is to learn how to speak while in a trance. When you speak from within a trance your entire demeanor is consistent with that trance and the listener virtually is compelled to enter into a trance with you in order to maintain congruity and to understand what you are saying.

As you imitate the demonstration by reading the transcript aloud, you automatically will begin to reenter a trance yourself. As you do so, continue reading the transcript with whatever voice tone, pacing or volume feels right to you or fits with your relaxed state of mind. Practice your own particular trance style until you are able to reproduce it whenever you wish.

3. While you are practicing your trance style, read the introduction to all of the remaining chapters and review the scripts presented in each. Please note, however, that the scripts themselves are not particularly informative or entertaining when read silently to oneself. In fact, they probably will seem somewhat silly, confusing or boring to you. Remember, these scripts were designed to minimize conscious awareness and to stimulate unconscious understandings and events during a trance, not to appeal to the conscious mind's critical faculties or aesthetic sensibilities.

Instead of reading these scripts silently to yourself, therefore, we strongly recommend that you and a colleague read them to each other. Take turns reading an induction script, a metaphor script, and the trance termination script to each other. If possible, tape record these practice sessions and review them together.

This procedure serves a dual purpose. It enables you to receive feedback regarding the effectiveness of your trance style as a hypnotherapist and it enables you to experience the effects of the various aspects of these scripts directly when you serve as the practice subject. *Such experiential practice sessions are the single most useful and efficient method of learning hypnotherapy.*

If you are unable to find a colleague to practice with, try listening to and participating with your own tape recordings of several induction and suggestion scripts. Though probably not as effective as working with a colleague, this approach can provide more of an appreciation for the content and structure of the scripts than can a straightforward reading of them.

4. We recommend that novice hypnotherapists begin practicing within a pain management context if possible. If this is feasible, focus your reading and practice on the material contained in Chapter 16 for a while.

5. Begin conducting Diagnostic Trance sessions with appropriate clients. This will help you get used to talking to people with their eyes closed and will provide the understanding needed to select appropriate scripts for each client. Postpone further hypnotherapeutic work until at least the next session, however, and use the intervening time to select and review the kinds of scripts you intend to use.

6. Conduct a hypnotherapy session with a client based upon the scripts you selected after doing a Diagnostic Trance. There is no need to be shy or coy about reading the material if that is what you choose to do. Clients usually are perfectly comfortable with this approach, especially if you indicate that you prefer to read material specifically selected for that client so that exactly the right words are used throughout. Take your time. Pay attention to the various reactions of the client as you proceed. Study the person carefully so that you can modify your approach in response to his/her reactions. Remember that each session typically will require:

   a) a transition into trance
   b) an induction to create a trance
   c) either a general metaphor or a specific diagnostic metaphor to stimulate therapeutic insights
   d) perhaps a direct suggestion or statement to stimulate change
   e) the trance termination procedure

7. Each session will last approximately 30 to 40 minutes depending upon which induction, metaphor and suggestion procedures are used. It usually is not necessary to explain the rationale or nature of the process. Just indicate that you would like to try something that might be of value and

interest, then proceed. Most clients seem to find the experience to be pleasant and interesting, even though it may be unusual and puzzling at first.

8. We would like to emphasize that the materials presented in this book are designed to serve as supplements to other sources of professional training. Mastery of these materials does not qualify anyone to practice hypnotherapy without additional supervision, reading and training in the field. Relevant workshops are offered on a regular basis to qualified mental health practitioners by various individuals and organizations. Persons who intend to use hypnotherapeutic techniques in their practice should contact the following organizations for more information:

> The American Society of Clinical Hypnosis
> 2250 East Devon Avenue, Suite 336
> Des Plaines, Illinois 60018

> The Society for Clinical and Experimental Hypnosis
> 128-A Kings Park Drive
> Liverpool, N.Y. 13090

> The Milton H. Erickson Foundation
> 3606 North 24th Street
> Phoenix, Arizona 85016

9. We also would like to emphasize that the scripts presented in this book should be used only by professionals who are qualified to make the kinds of observations and judgments necessary to use them with clinical sensitivity and acumen. There can be no guarantee that a given script will have the desired effect for everyone. Similarly, when used inappropriately or with inappropriate clients, hypnotherapy (like any therapeutic technique) could produce undesirable or counterproductive outcomes. In the final analysis, the decision to select and utilize all or part of a particular hypnotherapy script with a particular client is a judgment call which demands the utmost in clinical skill. Although we have found the material contained in these scripts to be useful and have published them here in the hope that others will find them equally beneficial, we cannot predict their impact when used by someone else nor can we assume responsibility for it. We suggest that you use these proce-

dures with the same degree of caution and care that you would any other intervention.

10. Over time you will develop a general sense of how to proceed and will become comfortable paraphrasing scripts or simply using them to stimulate ideas and to provide general guidelines. Eventually, the basic assessment and decision processes also will become so automatic that the material in this book will be superfluous. At that point you can relax and trust your own unconscious knowledge and understandings to guide you because you will have begun to *be* a hypnotherapist.

PART II

Scripts

3

—

TRANCE INDUCTION

Each induction script presented in this chapter has a different format and emphasis. One is designed for clients who have experienced hypnosis before, one is for people who are unable to remember ever having even one common, everyday trance experience and one never mentions hypnosis or trance at all. The last script is designed to teach clients how to induce trance in themselves.

These scripts also vary in length and complexity. Some are very brief and straightforward and a few are relatively long. Remember that it is not necessary to continue with a long trance induction once a trance has developed. As soon as the client demonstrates the *muscular relaxation, immobility, reduced breathing rate, slowed heart rate, reduced or eliminated swallow reflex, slowed eye movements,* and *quiet receptivity* characteristic of a light trance, it is appropriate to segue out of the trance induction and into the provision of ideas or metaphors designed to lead the client toward therapeutic awareness.

Please keep in mind the fact that these trance inductions can and do work. We have used these procedures successfully with hundreds of clients. Most people are able to learn how to enter into a trance state in only one or two sessions, especially if the therapist has a confident expectation that this will happen. Any concern about or lack of faith in the client's ability to enter into a trance will be conveyed to that person by subtle verbal and nonverbal cues, with negative results. On the other hand, confidence in the subject and in the procedures used will help insure a positive outcome. The role of confident expectation of therapeutic results is extremely powerful. In fact, it may be more significant than any other element of the hypnotherapeutic process.

On those rare occasions when an induction does not seem to help a client relax at all, the client should never be left with the impression that she/he has failed. Relaxation and trance are new and unusual experiences for most people and it may take time for them to adapt to the experience. As long as you maintain a positive expectation of success and reassure the client that she/he is doing well and that she/he eventually will be able to relax completely, that individual is likely to benefit from the process.

Also, please remember that trance is not a stable condition. Clients frequently drift in and out of trance in response to internal and external events. Should conscious arousal occur spontaneously, all you need to do is comment that drifting up and back down is fine. Then continue with whatever was being said prior to the arousal.

We advise you to review each script before you decide to use it. Although carefully worded to avoid problems and to elicit the desired trance, these scripts are designed to serve as guidelines, not as substitutes for your own creativity and style. Each may be modified or elaborated upon in any manner that seems comfortable to you.

INDUCTION SELECTION CRITERIA

Which type of induction script should you use with a specific client? Here are our recommendations:

Category I.   If your client has never experienced trance before and seems to be reasonably relaxed and cooperative, use the Basic Induction.

Category II.   If your client is compulsive, rigid or highly controlled, use the Confusion Induction.

Category III.   If your client is agitated, fearful or distractible, use a Conversational Induction.

Category IV.   If your client is a bit anxious and the room is noisy, use the Naturalistic Induction.

Category V.   If your client has experienced hypnosis before and that experience was positive, use the Revivification Induction.

Category VI.   If your client has never experienced a formal hypnosis process but can remember experiencing a trance-like state in some situation (e.g., jogging, meditating, driving), use the Simulation Induction.

Category VII.   If your client is looking for a demonstration of the power of hypnosis for reassurance or proof that it can and will help, use the Arm Levitation or Eye Closure Ratification Induction.

Category VIII.   If your client is an experienced subject who is willing and able to enter trance again, use one of the Brief Inductions.

Category IX.   If your goal is to help the person learn how to use self-hypnosis, use the Self-Hypnosis Training Process.

— OR —

If you are most comfortable with or confident in one of the inductions other than the one we have recommended, use it instead.

Before you begin to use any induction procedure, remember to initiate the process with an appropriate transition comment. Conversational Inductions can be conducted without an obvious transition, but we advise you to use one nonetheless.

NOTE: The scripts throughout this book are presented in a format that conveys the intended rhythm and phrasing. A pause between each line establishes a rhythmic presentation conducive to trance, gives emphasis to specific words or ideas, and gives the client time to experience internal events relevant to those words and ideas. During the first part of any induction procedure, each line should be spoken in synchrony with the client's exhalations. After the first few lines, however, the pace should be slowed gradually until a rhythm of presentation is reached which seems to be appropriate for or compatible with the relaxed state of trance. Once established, this basic rhythm of presentation can be used throughout the hypnotherapy process.

CATEGORY I: BASIC INDUCTION SCRIPT

Applications: For use with cooperative clients who never have experienced trance before. The purpose is to inform them about the process of trance and to initiate trance experiences.

That's right!
With your eyes closed
you can begin to relax,
though at first
you may be more aware of some things
than you were before.
The sounds in the room,
the sound of my voice,
sensations in hands or feet,
thoughts and images
that drift into the mind automatically.
Because,
with the eyes closed
it becomes easier and easier,
to become more and more aware,
of a variety of things
that otherwise would go overlooked,
or ignored.
Thoughts,
feelings,
sensations,
and the alteration
of awareness
as the mind begins to experience
that gradual letting go.
Letting go even
of the effort it takes
to be aware
of exactly where
the arms are positioned
or the hands,
or fingers.
And even the effort it takes
to be aware
of which leg
seems to relax more quickly, or completely
than the other
may seem to be

too much effort
to bother making.
But it takes time
to experience that letting go.
Your own time,
in your own way,
as you begin to learn
even more than before
about your own ability to relax,
and let go,
and the mind
begins to flow
down
toward that place
of quietness
and calm awareness.
A place
that almost seems
to give off signals
that direct awareness down,
toward it,
into it
more. . . .
and more completely.
A place of effortless relaxation
and letting go,
where even the effort it takes
to be aware
of the sound of my voice
or the meaning of my words
may almost seem to be
too much effort
to bother making.
It's so much easier
simply to relax
and to allow events to occur
almost by themselves.
A drifting down,

and a drifting back
upwards,
toward the surface of wakeful awareness at
    times,
and that's fine.
It all belongs
to you.
Because you have a conscious mind,
and an unconscious mind,
and that unconscious mind,
the back of the mind,
can continue to hear,
to understand,
and to respond,
to those things I might say
without the need for you
to do anything at all.
It's so much easier
for the conscious mind
to be able to relax
and to enjoy
that drifting down,
into that place
of quiet calmness,
and effortless awareness,
of many different things,
without needing to make an effort
even to remember
exactly how
to make the effort it might take
to tell the exact position
of arms,
or legs,
or the entire body,
that seems to float
in time and space—
that free-floating place
of effortless letting go
and allowing events to occur
in their own time,
and in their own way.
That's right. . . .
The unconscious mind
can allow that drifting

to occur,
while the conscious mind
drifts off
someplace else entirely now.
That's right.
In your own time,
in your own way,
aware of events
that occur along the way,
as the unconscious mind
begins to utilize
that opportunity
to alter your experience
and to continue that learning
in whatever way
is the right way
for you.
Learning that feeling
of letting go,
of allowing the unconscious mind
to assume more and more
responsibility
for guiding and directing awareness
as you continue
to explore
your own abilities
and capacities
to learn as you relax,
as you relax
and enter into that trance
more and more completely,
more and more comfortably,
more and more effortlessly
than before.
That's right.
[*Go to selected metaphor script or trance
termination procedure.*]

CATEGORY II: CONFUSION INDUCTION SCRIPT

Applications: For use with highly intellectualized or rigidly controlled individuals whose conscious minds would continue to analyze, critique, plan, etc. throughout a basic induction or for whom letting go of control is a concern. This script is not recommended for persons who are suspicious or paranoid.
(The initial part of this script should be presented rather rapidly, with a gradual slowing down into a more typical trance induction rhythm.)

Now,
before you begin,
I should say,
how glad I am
to be working with you today,
instead of a dull-witted mind,
the kind you might find,
in the gutter someplace
arguing with everyone,
mad at the world.
Because when I see them,
they keep shifting around,
scratching itches,
never getting comfortable,
thinking they know it all,
and no one
can tell them what to do,
not even to help them
and they refuse to learn
anything that might get them
to climb out of that place
and take care of themselves.
So it is nice to know
that anyone with your intelligence
can easily learn
how to drift into trance.
So you can sit there,
in that chair,
here,
while you try,
to be aware,
of the exact meaning
of the words you hear
and of all the changes
that occur there
in your thoughts,
sensations
or awareness
as I speak here.
Or you can forget
to try
to make
the effort it takes
to pay close attention
to everything that happens
or does not happen
in your experience
as you listen to me
and also to your own thoughts,
or to your sensations
that change over time,
or stay the same,
in an arm or an ear,
and your legs or fingers.
And what about the thoughts,
and the variety of images,
that speak to your mind's eye
as I speak to your mind
and what you speak
to yourself
speaks for itself
as you try to search
and find
that things
may seem to be one thing,
but turn out to be another.
Because two and two
are four,
but two can also
mean also

and no two are alike.
It all belongs
to you
and to your own ability
to relax
those two ears too,
and to begin to know,
that you really don't know
what means yes
and what means no, here,
though you may
try to guess
where you're going
to go,
you don't know
that there is no
real way to know
how to let go
while holding on
and to recognize
that there is nothing
you need to try to know,
to do,
or not do,
because everything you do
allows you
to recognize that I can say
many different things
and there is no need
for you to make
the effort it takes
to try to make
the effort
to pay close attention
to each thing I say
or don't say,
because there was a time
when the effort
to train
the mind
to stay on track
was not worth
the trip
that led the mind

back to that time
of peaceful,
calm awareness,
of effortless
letting go,
and knowing,
that you don't need
to try
to hear,
or to understand
what I might say
later on here.
The conscious mind,
can go anywhere it wishes,
while I continue
to talk
and your unconscious mind
continues to hear,
the way you overhear
a conversation.
You don't even need
to do anything at all.
It all belongs to you,
as you begin to hear,
the way you do,
here and now,
with eyes closed,
comfortable,
that voice or sound,
in the background,
of the mind,
as you listened
to that show,
and felt
the relaxed
drifting
glow
of a slow,
sound
show
of quiet
calmness
and thoughts,
like dreams,

followed themselves
as I spoke,
turning,
spokes in a wheel,
turning,
drifting,
effortlessly down
into a quiet,
still place,
where words
can remind
your mind
of those things
needed
for you.
[*Go to a metaphor or to trance termination.*]

CATEGORY III: CONVERSATIONAL INDUCTION SCRIPT

Applications: For use with clients who are anxious about the hypnotic process or who might be reluctant to engage in hypnosis per se. This induction procedure does not mention trance or hypnosis. Instead it focuses upon the development of relaxation and comfortable self-awareness. Obtain the client's permission to help him/her learn how to relax more fully before you begin. Once the client has learned how to relax completely, reorient him/her to wakeful awareness and then obtain permission to conduct a hypnotherapeutic session. This procedure avoids any impression of deceit or trickery and is an honest demonstration of respect for the client's autonomy.

I know that sometimes
it is difficult
to *relax*
or to learn how
to *relax* more
than you have before.
And so,
as you sit there
with your eyes closed,
and begin to become aware
of your own thoughts,
of your own sensations,
I begin to wonder
if you have ever
had the *pleasure*
of sitting on the bank
of a river,
or on the shore
of a lake or ocean.
Because there is something
very *comforting*
about just sitting there,
listening to the *peaceful* sound
of the waves,
as they move in,
and out,
in a continuous flow,
that just seems to go on and on.
Relaxing in the sun,
feeling the *soothing* warmth,
and just letting the mind drift,
effortlessly,

with that quiet, almost silent,
sound,
in the background of awareness.
I'm not even sure
you've ever done that before,
relaxed in that way,
listening to the *peaceful quietness,*
of water washing the shore.
Perhaps it was a waterfall,
or just a silent place
in the center of a woods,
a *happy* memory of *contentment,*
or just a dream . . .
of a place so *comfortable* and *safe,*
that it was *easy*
to allow the body
to *relax,*
everything
to *relax.*
I don't know,
but I do know
that *everyone* has a place
they can go,
a relaxing space
deep down inside
where they can *really let go*
of all their cares and concerns,
and wonder at the wonder
of those waves of relaxation,
at the smooth *heaviness*
of arms and legs
as *relaxation* continues.

Maybe it was the warm *smoothness*
of the soft white sand,
you could hold in your hand
and watch *flow effortlessly*
through your fingers,
the same sand
that flows in an hourglass,
hour after hour,
with nothing to do for a time,
except *let go* and flow,
warm, heavy sand,
listening to the *waves*
of relaxation,
secure inside and out,
while you were sitting there,
by the shore
forgetting to make
the effort it takes
even to try
to be aware
of when
or where
that *relaxation* began
and the *soothing* sounds
or sensations were.
[*Either continue with a different
induction or awaken the client and
discuss his/her progress in relaxing.*]

CATEGORY IV: NATURALISTIC INDUCTION SCRIPT

Application: For anxious subjects and/or a noisy environment. Because of the content of this induction, it should not be used with anyone who is afraid of water.

You're resting in the chair,
with your eyes closed,
and you may notice your eyes,
even wish to open them from time to time,
and that's fine,
because I really wouldn't want you
to not go into a trance too quickly.
So much easier
simply to allow
that feeling in a shoulder, in a hand . . .
to continue as you listen
to the sounds of my voice
the sounds in the room,
the sounds outside the room,
other voices, other rooms,
while you pay close attention
to the changes in an arm, a hand,
and wonder if you are going
to be able to go
into a trance
while your conscious mind
has already begun to drift down
to let go for a time,
allowing the body to relax the mind
to relax with it
without knowing at times
how much more comfortable
you really can become.
And sooner or later
everyone's had the experience
of falling asleep
while watching television,
paying close attention
to the story line
just closing the eyes a moment
to rest quietly,
hearing the music,
listening to the voices
in that comfortably relaxed way,

when a word or a phrase
reminds you of a particular memory,
and you drift,
dream away for a time . . .
come back to the words again,
drift, dream away again . . .
until the words
and the music
become a soothing sound
in the background of the mind
just for a time,
and the unconscious mind
continues to hear
everything of importance to you,
while the conscious mind
may not notice
that you need not listen
to everything I say.
Because you've known all along
how much easier it is
to learn something when you're relaxed . . .
though I wouldn't want you
to relax too deeply at first,
so much more important
for you to recognize the small changes,
tiny changes, barely noticeable,
happening in your breathing . . .
in your pulse . . .
in the relaxation of the face,
in a feeling of comfort . . . security.
Because your unconscious will choose
to relax your little finger
before those feelings begin in a thumb,
or perhaps your wrist
will be the handiest place
to begin relaxing,
but the conscious mind can enjoy
being curious about exactly where
those feelings will begin.

If you drop a pebble
into a pool of water
the water flows in ripples on the surface,
but just below the surface . . .
just beneath the surface of awareness,
the pebble drifts
down. . . .
And as that pebble drifts down,
past the water animals, . . .
drifting down past the water plants,
gently floating down . . .
nothing is disturbed
as it slowly comes to rest
on the bottom of the quiet pool.
Even the surface ripples
become slower and quieter,
and beneath the surface
all is still, calm. . . .
And you can recognize your ability
to relax and comfortably reflect
upon your problems in a certain way,
remembering those times
when you were sure things were one way
and they turned out
to be something else entirely.
Perhaps as a child,
learning that liberry
is really library,
or telling the difference
between feet and feat,
changing old beliefs,
learning new meanings,
new ways of doing things.
And I wonder if those new feelings,
those hypnotic feelings
will stay the same
or continue to deepen even more
as you try to remember
everything I've said to you
about those TV dreams
and pebbles that drift down,
sometimes more quickly,
sometimes very slowly . . .
[*Go to metaphor script or trance termina-*
tion process.]

CATEGORY V: REVIVIFICATION INDUCTION SCRIPT

Application: For use with clients who have successfully experienced hypnosis before. The goal is to enable the client to reexperience trance by remembering what it was like on that previous occasion.

As you continue to relax,
with your eyes closed,
listening to the sound of my voice,
you may begin to remember
those experiences of hypnosis
that you have had before.
How it felt to listen
to that voice,
speaking to you . . .
Remembering that sound
and the words . . .
as you began
to drift down.
That feeling
in your hands
or legs
or arms,
That feeling of relaxation, perhaps,
and what you thought
as you began to enter
that deep trance state.
The sensations
and images,
the alterations
in awareness,
as your conscious mind
became more and more
comfortable
and your unconscious mind,
assumed more and more
responsibility
for guiding and directing
thoughts
and responses.
Remembering
where you were,
in what position,
what you did,

what was said to you,
how you felt
as you learned to allow
that trance to continue.
And even now,
as you continue
to reexperience
the memory
of that event,
and to allow those feelings
to become a part
of your experience now . . .
I would like you
to have the opportunity
to enjoy
allowing
that trance to continue
as you drift deeper
and deeper
and my voice
drifts with you,
to become a part
of your experience
as you become
more deeply relaxed
and comfortable
in that trance
and I continue to
talk to you.
[*Go to selected metaphor or to trance termination.*]

CATEGORY VI: SIMULATION INDUCTION SCRIPT

Application: For use with clients who can remember a non-hypnotic trance experience they have had in a particular situation such as jogging, sitting by the ocean, etc. Information about this experience should be obtained prior to the induction and incorporated into it where appropriate.

You are sitting there. . . .
Your eyes are closed . . .
You are hearing
many different sounds
including the sound
of my voice.
And I really do not know
how you are aware
of your hands resting there,
or your legs,
or your feet.
But I do know
that some muscles
can feel more relaxed
than others
as you continue listening
to my words
and become more
and more comfortable
becoming more deeply hypnotized.
Because you are
breathing in . . .
and breathing out . . .
And you are able
to be aware
of many different sensations . . .
and thoughts. . . .
including those thoughts,
images
and sensations
that come to mind
in response to my words.
So, as I continue
to say things to you . . .
and you continue
to be more aware
of some things than others,

it may become easier and easier
for you to begin
to remember
particular things
about your experiences
while [*jogging, reading, or
whatever the person specifically
mentioned that has absorbed
attention or created a trance
in the past*].
Because even though
you are sitting
in this room
you can begin to imagine
the experience of [*jogging, reading, etc.,
as above*],
can you not?
You can return your attention
to that experience
and begin to remember
many different things
about it.
You may be able
to feel [*insert something usually felt in that
      situation*].
You may be able
to see [*insert something usually seen
      in that situation*].
You may be able
to hear [*insert something usually
      heard in that situation*].
In fact,
you may be able to experience
so many different things
that it almost seems as if
you can return to that experience
quite completely.

And even as you continue . . .
to enjoy those feelings
of deep relaxation
and comfortable letting go,
of becoming more and more
a part of that experience,
I can continue
to speak to you now,
and you can allow
my words
to drift through your mind
as your unconscious mind
allows you
to experience those things needed.
[*Go to selected metaphor, direct
suggestion, or trance termination.*]

CATEGORY VIIA: ARM LEVITATION RATIFICATION INDUCTION SCRIPT

Application: For use with clients who expect or are seeking a demonstration of hypnosis or who might benefit from the experience of an unconscious alteration of behavior or sensation. This approach helps to validate hypnosis as a real and potentially influential phenomenon.

[*This induction works better if the client is sitting upright rather than reclining or lying down.*]

The first thing
I would like you to do,
before you continue
to relax
and enter into a trance,
is to place the very tips
of your fingers very lightly
on your thighs,
with your arms in the air,
elbows away from your sides,
as if your arms and hands
were just floating there,
fingers just barely touching the cloth,
so you can just feel the texture.
That's right!
Fingers just barely touching,
and focus your full attention
on those sensations
in the very tips of those fingers,
where they just barely touch,
where that floating continues.
Because,
as I talk to you
and you continue to relax,
and to pay close attention,
to those sensations,
an interesting thing is beginning to happen.
Because everyone knows
how easy it is
to learn something
when you're comfortable.
And sooner or later
everyone has the experience
of learning something new
when they're relaxed.
So go ahead and allow
that comfortable feeling
to continue
with the recognition
that after a while
you can notice
that your unconscious mind
has begun to gently lift up one hand
or the other, or both.
It may be difficult to hold it there,
just barely touching your leg,
as it keeps trying
to move upwards a bit
as it feels lighter,
and lighter,
and lifts upwards,
drifts upwards,
almost by itself at times
And the other
may seem to get heavier,
difficult to tell the difference
at first,
but as you pay close attention,
it becomes easier,
and easier,
to notice which seems heavier,
and which seems lighter.
And when you begin
to notice which hand seems heavier,
you may let it relax
and come to rest
in a comfortable place
while you pay more and more attention
to that other hand,
to that light lifting upwards hand,

that moves up a bit at times,
and then back down perhaps,
and then back upwards again.
And after a while
you may begin to notice
that you can allow
that drifting upwards
to continue . . .
more and more upwards,
lighter, floating upwards
as you allow that movement
to continue on and on,
an automatic movement upwards
as your unconscious mind
lifts that hand, that arm, upwards,
one step at a time,
upwards and then more and more.
It may be difficult
to tell exactly how much
that arm and hand have drifted up,
to tell exactly
what position they are in,
and it may be difficult to tell
when that slow effortless movement
occurs more and more rapidly,
as it drifts up,
lighter and lighter,
higher and higher.
That's right. [*Pause for upward movement.*]
That's right.
And that arm and hand
could continue to drift higher
and get lighter and lighter,
but as you pay close attention to it,
you may begin to notice
how it feels now,
how tired and heavy it is,
as your unconscious mind
reminds your mind,
to pay more and more attention
to that heaviness pulling down.
And that arm can begin
to move down now,
as that heaviness increases,

and it would be so comfortable,
just to allow
that heavy arm to drift down now.
That's right,
drifting down
moving it down now,
letting it return
to a comfortable resting position
where it can relax completely,
and you can relax completely,
drifting down with it,
down into a deep, deep trance,
as your arm relaxes
and the mind relaxes as well,
and you drift deeper and deeper
as I continue to talk,
and your arms and hands
feel so comfortable,
your entire body comfortable,
comfortable and relaxed.
That's right.
[*Go to metaphor or a trance termination procedure.*]

CATEGORY VIIB: EYE CLOSURE RATIFICATION INDUCTION SCRIPT

Application: Like the Arm Levitation Induction, this script is designed to elicit an unconscious pattern of responses to hypnotic suggestions which will ratify or validate hypnosis as a real phenomenon. The purpose is to convince the person at a conscious level that something unusual or different and potentially very useful is happening to his/her state of mind.

[*Obviously, the client should leave his/her eyes open for this induction procedure. Stop the induction and move on to a metaphor or a trance termination if the client's eyes close before the end of the script.*]

As you sit there
and let yourself get comfortable,
you can look at [*pick a point or an object which the subject must look upwards slightly to see*].
That's right,
just let your eyes rest there,
looking at that particular spot,
and continue to relax.
Because as you relax
and look at that spot there,
you can begin to notice
any changes that occur here.
You can notice any blurring,
or the difficulty of focusing,
of holding your eyes there,
looking at that one place,
though at first
it may be difficult
to recognize those changes here
as you attempt to try
to be unaware of them
or to keep staring at that spot,
using all of your effort
to hold your eyes there.
But after a while
you may begin to notice
the effort it takes
to try to be unaware
of those changes that occur . . .

just a little at first,
that slight blurring of vision,
the heavy tiredness in the eyes,
or the way the spot seems to move about,
or changes shape, or color,
and your eyes become more and more tired,
tired and heavy,
that tired heavy feeling
that you have felt before
as you stared at something
and your eyes began to water
and began to want to close,
to blink closed,
to want to stay closed,
and rest that tiredness.
That's right,
because everybody knows
how it feels
when the eyes get tired,
as the body relaxes
and the mind relaxes,
so tired and heavy
and the eyes begin to close.
Everybody knows,
how much more comfortable it would be
to allow the eyes to close.
That's right,
because after a while
they have become
so tired and heavy
they almost seem to close
by themselves.
And your eyes *can close*,
and as they *close*
you can feel
that heavy, tired relaxation

begin to spread
throughout the entire body,
the arms,
the face,
the legs,
and the mind relaxes as well.
With the eyes closed
the entire body can relax
and you can drift down
into a deep, sound sleep,
a comfortable relaxed trance,
where I can talk to you,
and your unconscious mind
can listen
even as your conscious mind
drifts off
in the same effortless way,
that the eyes drift closed
and relax.
[*If the subject's eyes are closed,
go to a metaphor or a trance
termination process. If his/her
eyes are still open, continue
with the next few sentences.*]
So go ahead now and allow
the eyes to close.
That's right, close your eyes *now*
and the mind relaxes.
As you continue
to drift deeper and deeper
into a relaxed trance
and I continue
to talk.
[*Go to metaphor script or trance
termination.*]

CATEGORY VIII: BRIEF INDUCTION SCRIPTS

Applications: For use with experienced subjects or for the creation of light trances such as those used for diagnostic purposes.

A.

Now,
as you sit there,
with your eyes closed,
and begin to drift
into trance,
in your own way,
in your own time,
you can take your time
to allow

that letting go to occur.
[*Pause while relaxation and trance develop.*]
Because your conscious mind
can do anything it wishes,
while your unconscious mind
continues to hear,
and to understand,
those things I might say.
[*Go to selected metaphor script.*]

B.

Now,
as you relax
and begin to remember
the experience of trance,
you can reexperience
those changes,
in thought feeling and sensation
and drift down

into that trance
even more comfortably
and effortlessly
than before.
[*Pause for trance to develop.*]
That's right.
[*Go to selected metaphor script.*]

C.

Relaxing
drifting down,
letting go,
allowing thoughts
to drift,
images to appear,
and not needing to do anything at all.
[*Pause*]

Not even needing
to wonder
what you will learn
as my voice
drifts down
with you.
[*Go to selected metaphor script.*]

D.

And you
can allow
that feeling
of trance

now . . .
[*Pause*]
[*Go to selected metaphor script.*]

CATEGORY IX: SELF-HYPNOSIS TRAINING SCRIPT

Applications: For training clients how to enter and use a self-hypnotic trance. This process should be used only with individuals who have entered trance several times before.

Today,
as you drift into your trance,
I would like to help you learn
even more than before
about how to allow
this alteration to occur
anytime at all
that you need to
or want to.
That's right,
because today
you can drift into that trance
in a different way,
all by yourself.
And you can learn
how to drift into that trance
for a brief time,
or a long time,
anytime, anywhere
that is useful to you
to be able to utilize
your own unconscious mind
to do so many things
for you.
And so,
before you drift down completely,
what I would like you to do
is to make a fist
with your right
or your left hand.
That's right,
a tight fist
with that hand.
And pay very close attention
to the tightness in that hand,
in the fingers,
in the back of the hand,
in the muscles of the forearm,
as you feel that tightness.
And now

you can relax that hand
and pay close attention
to that relaxation
as it occurs
more and more completely,
and that heaviness begins to spread
up through the arm
into the shoulder,
and the back,
and the other arm.
That's right.
And that relaxation
can continue to increase
as your legs relax,
and your neck relaxes
and your face relaxes,
as you relax everyplace,
and continue to drift down,
more and more completely,
more and more deeply
into that trance state of mind,
where the mind relaxes as well,
and it becomes
easier and easier
just to allow
the unconscious mind
to assume more and more responsibility
for guiding and directing awareness
and providing those experiences
that are useful to you.
That's right,
you can continue
to drift down quite effortlessly
and you can drift upwards as well,
up toward the surface of awareness
where you can have the opportunity
to practice that ability
to create your own trance
experience.
And as you drift back now

to the surface of wakeful awareness,
you can make that tight fist again . . .
[*Wait for the subject to make a fist again.*]
And you can pay attention again
to that tightness
and to the spreading relaxation
as you relax that hand
and feel that drifting back down,
drifting back down into that trance
in your own time,
in your own way.
And I would like you
to continue to experience
that ability to drift down
on your own
as I sit here
quietly for a while
and you continue to learn
how to let go in that way
and I just sit here with you
for a while.
That's right.
[*Pause for at least a minute,
unless the subject begins to
reawaken, then continue.*]
And so you have learned,
how to make that fist,
and how to relax that hand
and drift down with that relaxation,
into your own trance state,
an effortless state
of not needing to do
anything at all
as you let go
more and more completely
and drift down and back up
in your own time
and in your own way,
in whatever way
your unconscious mind knows
is the right way for you.
Because as you learned
how to drift down
in that way,

your unconscious mind
becomes more and more available
to you now.
And anytime, anywhere you wish
you can utilize that ability . . .
you can make a tight fist,
you can drift down into trance
with the understanding
that your unconscious mind
can do those things needed.
All you need to do
is to let go completely
with the thought or idea
of providing an opportunity
for your unconscious mind
to take care of those things
for *you.*
All you need to do
is to ask it to do so
as you drift down
and then drift back upwards
now,
in your own way
in your own time, . . .
back toward the surface
of wakeful awareness
and alertness
bringing those learnings
with you.
That's right,
back to wakeful alertness now
with a relaxed, refreshed feeling
of comfortable self-awareness.
And as you reach the surface
of wakeful awareness,
you can allow
the eyes
to open
now.
[*After the subject becomes reoriented, it is
helpful to immediately have him/her practice
the self-induction process again once or
twice. This solidifies the learning and makes
it a skill available to the conscious mind.*]

4

——

GENERAL PURPOSE METAPHORS

The metaphors and anecdotes (actually metaphorical anecdotes) presented in this chapter can be used with virtually any client. They are designed to convey universally applicable messages about the nature and source of therapeutic change and to stimulate the use of inner resources for self-healing.

We recommend that you use one or two of these general purpose metaphors during the first hypnotherapy session. If therapeutic benefits are not apparent by the following session, you may wish to begin using the symptom or problem-specific metaphors presented in later chapters and perhaps the direct statements about therapeutic change presented in Chapter 14. Initially, however, it is best to introduce clients to the hypnotherapeutic process via general purpose metaphors such as these. They are relatively nonthreatening and thus establish a comfortable familiarity with the hypnotherapeutic procedure.

You may select whatever script you believe will capture the interest and attention of your client or use the script that is most comfortable for you. Because these are general purpose metaphors, there are no specific reasons for choosing one over another aside from individual preferences and tastes.

As with the induction scripts, we have attempted to present these scripts in a format that conveys a rhythm and phrasing consistent with a trance state. Nonetheless, as with the induction scripts, it is not absolutely necessary for you to read them verbatim to your clients. Feel free to embellish them or to change the wording in whatever way you like.

BUILDING A HOUSE

It can be very relaxing
to watch someone working.
Educational as well.
And I wonder
if you know
what is involved
in building a house, home,
a place to live, to be.
I don't know
everything involved,
but I remember watching,
as a child,
the way they marked it off
with stakes at each corner
on the vacant lot
and then dug the foundation,
deep in the soil,
and poured truckloads of concrete,
for the basement floor,
and the thick walls,
reinforced with steel bars,
to prevent cracking
or crumbling.
That house
was built to last.
A solid foundation
to rest upon,
to build the rest of a life upon.
And as you rest there,
continuing to relax,
your unconscious mind
can use that time
to examine closely
the foundation
of thought,
ideas,
beliefs,
values,
of experiences
defined by the blueprint,
the design,
of what is wanted

and where it is built,
already or planned.
Because someone
had to foresee
to see in the mind's eye,
what was to be,
what would be
how it would look,
where it would sit,
how it would function,
that house,
sitting there,
a place to live,
a place to be,
for someone to enter,
and relax comfortably,
welcomed
and protected within,
arranged and organized,
for living within.
So if the walls
could talk
they would soothe,
and observe
a smooth, effortless flow
from one room to another,
one space to another,
a living space,
living room,
the private places,
private rooms,
where private events,
and private thoughts,
can occur safely,
and be kept
safe and sound.
Where a child
could go,
to explore and examine
room after room,
floor after floor,
hidden spaces,

crawl spaces,
storage places,
full of memories,
and things put away until later.
Some remembered,
some forgotten,
old toys, school papers, pictures and books
some used, some ignored,
each with a feeling,
that also was stored.
A house full of places,
empty spaces,
to be filled
and transformed
to meet the needs,
the desires,
of those who choose
to live within,
within oneself,
to weather the storms,
to work on ideas
to let the mind wander,
gazing out at the sky,
or the people walking by
or coming in, and sharing and talking.
And as I talk
that solid foundation takes form
the ground floor takes shape.
The plans that tell
where things go,
how things will be,
what and where
is the key.
A key question,
what will be done,
what are the plans
that guide and provide
a solid foundation to build upon
for the future.
All from a few stakes
that mark out the place
where they dig a hole
deep down
in the ground,

where something was once,
but is now replaced
by a new place to be,
a new space to see,
a relaxed place to be
even now as you relax even more
and drift in thoughts
about what will be
and what was found
that can be used later on.
Because I don't know,
what your unconscious mind knows,
or what it shows you,
when you wander and wonder
what you want,
what you will be
what it will take for you
to live comfortably here and there,
but you can know,
or begin to know,
now. . . .
[*Go to trance termination.*]

THE PLANE TRIP

And there are
different ways of relaxing
and taking a trip someplace else.
You can watch the passengers
pass the time waiting
for a plane to board.
It is plain to see
that some are excited,
some are bored,
and some use the time
to see what they can see.
Some sleep in their chairs,
some watch their watches closely,
anxiously wondering
when they'll get where they're going
while others relax
and enjoy the opportunity
to have nothing to do
except relax and learn.
And it's plain to see
even before they've boarded the plane
and left the ground
who will enjoy the trip
and who will worry
all the way there.
Some help the pilot
get off the ground,
they shift around in their seats,
lifting the plane,
not trusting that hidden voice
that announces the altitude,
or the co-pilot,
or the plane, itself,
to get them there.
Always worrying,
worrying in all ways,
whether this drifting down . . .
or back up . . .
is normal and safe
while someplace else,
another mind sits,
passing the time relaxing,

thinking things through,
or looking out the window
at the scene below
as the fields and farms
drift by below
where the farmers plow and sow
and plan ahead and know
that some things
can't be helped,
that there are some things
they *can* do
and other things they cannot,
and that worrying
about the weather
won't make it rain,
but that pulling on the reins,
can stop a horse in time.
And so at night they sit back
in a comfortable chair
and relax wondering
at the wonder of it all,
and learn to trust
themselves,
what they know,
what they do.
And that person can see,
all that and more
from that view above it all
relaxed, barely aware
of where they are
in space and time.
While someplace else,
another mind can decide
what to do and when,
the right way at the right time,
for *you*.
To relax and enjoy the view,
to do what you can,
to look down within
and discover
how much more there is
than there was before

to you, within you,
to utilize in whatever way
is the right way
for you
to do those things needed.
That's right. . . .
Go ahead and take some time,
your own time,
to watch and learn and decide.
[*Go to trance termination.*]

ERICKSON'S WISDOM

And so, while you relax
I can wonder,
as I often do,
what that master hypnotherapist,
Milton Erickson,
would say to you, now.
Because he often had his clients relax,
and he spoke to them of many things
while they drifted into a deep trance
and became aware of things
that otherwise would go overlooked,
or ignored,
or hidden from view.
Because he almost seemed
to see into their minds,
to see through them, into them,
where they kept hidden
their secret hopes, dreams and fears.
And he knew what to say,
what to do,
to help them learn to use
their hidden talents,
their hidden knowledge,
to get them to face
what they tried to ignore,
to get them to do
what they needed to do
but would rather pretend
they could not.
He always found some way around
their usual ways of hiding
by telling them stories
about things he knew
or about childhood experiences
full of symbols and signs.
And they always knew
that he was talking to them,
showing them things,
teaching them things,
that they needed to know
but didn't know they knew,
or knew but were saying no to
even though it was not new to them.

And so,
I imagine he would talk to you
about the unconscious mind,
those thoughts and ideas
that come into view
as you relax
and begin to become aware,
that somewhere in there
are memories and learnings
and things you know
and things you can do.
If only he were here
to talk to you,
because I don't know,
but you do know,
the things he might say,
the things he might do
to point out to you,
those memories and abilities,
to help you decide
what to do and how.
A wise old man
who was not afraid
to help others see themselves
to help others accept
responsibility
for doing what was right.
A wise old man
who could talk to you
about what you knew as a child,
running and playing
or watching clouds,
how hard it was
to learn those things,
to resist some things,
to do the right things,
and how good it felt
when you felt or knew
that you were in charge of you.
But I'll save my stories,
and you can save yours,
for those times at night,
drifting in dreams,

when the mind relaxes
and images flow
and knowing occurs that changes things
that reveals things unseen and unheard before.
And in some unknown way
you'll know that he knew
and said to you
what you needed to hear,
what you needed to know,
because something changes,
rearranges,
in the mind's eye view
and you begin to do things — differently,
to experience things — differently,
to face things — differently,
to be able to do
what you could not do before.
You know and I know
that you know
that it all belongs
to you.
To hold on
or to let go,
to move on
or to stay put,
to put on
or to take off on your own,
or to change those things that you do
to avoid doing what you need to do
to change what is happening to you,
within you,
around you,
because it all belongs
to *you.* . . .
[*Go to trance termination.*]

THE MIGRATION OF IDEAS

And even as you relax more and more,
the mind automatically moves toward
those thoughts, ideas, images
that clarify most clearly for you,
the very things you know and do
that seem to get in the way.
Awareness migrates toward
things that need attention,
in the same way animals migrate.
Automatically,
without thinking or trying,
they seem to know
when to go and where,
and what to do to take care of themselves.
An inner voice, an inner awareness
that moves the birds,
the butterflies,
the whales,
the herds of animals
from one place to another,
that makes them restless,
something not right,
that draws their attention
toward that uncomfortable feeling
and sets them in motion,
moving toward a place,
perhaps the ocean,
an inner space,
of quiet comfort
and effortless relaxation.
And they move
hundreds of miles, thousands of miles,
taking care of their young,
taking care of themselves.
And no one really knows,
exactly how it feels
to be an otter, or a whale, or a butterfly,
that suddenly knows
the time is right
for a change,
that suddenly knows
the exact change needed.
But we can relax and imagine

how it might feel
to gradually or suddenly recognize that
    feeling,
that inner awareness,
that restless recognition,
that something needs to change
and needs to change now.
And we can imagine
how it might feel
to know without knowing
what needs to be done,
to be told without hearing,
by an inner voice, an inner feeling,
to do this *now*.
And we can imagine,
how it might feel
to have actions flow
from those feelings,
responding effortlessly, automatically,
to that inner awareness, that inner
    knowing,
that tells us what to do
and when
and how to do it.
To be born
with that knowledge,
to trust that feeling,
to be so comfortably aware of oneself,
that everything becomes easier,
though no one ever imagined
that traveling a thousand miles
is easy,
even though the decision to go
seemed to take no effort at all.
A decision, a knowing
that is a part of each being
that guides and directs automatically
toward those things needed.
A migration of thought,
of awareness.
which presents memories, ideas,
    understandings,
 for you to use

for you.
That's right.
Even as you relax
and drift toward those things needed,
the unconscious mind
automatically provides that awareness
that you can use later on
or right now.
[*Go to trance termination.*]

VACATIONS

And anytime
you drift off someplace else . . .
it is like a vacation,
going off someplace different.
You experience different things . . .
and forget for a time
the cares and concerns . . .
and discover something new
or remember something old, forgotten.
Because it is comforting to let go
and to enjoy that new way of seeing,
that new way of being
that you can experience . . .
like the woman I know who traveled alone
down to Florida.
She'd never been out of the Midwest;
but as soon as she got off the plane
she began to experience
new things . . .
and she began to change
her way of thinking,
her way of being.
The warm salt sea breeze
brushed her skin
with its new smell,
the palm trees caught her eye,
the sand glistened in the sun
and she felt strange,
alive and alert to every new thing,
new sights, sounds, smells,
new ways of doing things.
She walked on the beach
where she stopped and talked
to many new people . . .
from many different places
and she felt her world,
her inner world,
expand . . .
as she became aware
of how much more there is
than she knew before.
She saw every detail
of every shell, plant and form
of every brightly painted home,
and she began to make friends . . .
people from all over the world
with new ideas,
new ways of speaking,
new places to show her,
new experiences to share.
This shy Midwest farm girl,
had her eyes opened,
her mind opened,
to a whole new world.
Because everything was so different
she couldn't ignore it,
she couldn't deny it.
Even while swimming in the ocean
she continued to learn,
that things are not always
what they seem,
or may seem to be one thing
but turn out to be another,
like the strange things she felt
as she walked through the water,
and her mind could imagine
what lurked beneath the surface
tickling her feet, wrapping around her legs
with strange and frightening sensations.
But when she really looked
to see what was there,
it was beautiful sea grasses
rolling with the waves,
and soft fern mosses,
not the stuff of her imagination
not what she had feared,
just something wonderfully new . . .
like the new thoughts she had,
the new feelings she felt,
as she relaxed on the beach
and let her mind go,
let her mind wander deep down below,
where things go overlooked or ignored or
        unused.

Those deep down thoughts
began to bubble up,
to drift up into her awareness.
She began to think things
she had never thought before,
to know things
she's never allowed herself
to know before.
She began to remember things . . .
new things about old times,
old things in new ways
good times and bad times,
in good ways and bad ways.
She discovered treasures
buried deep inside,
she experienced pleasures
she had always denied.
She let herself *know*,
though it was hard at times,
and took a long time
to look at it all
in all ways
so that she would always know
what it was she knew
and what she needed to do
now that she knew
so many new things.
She returned home
but she never forgot what she learned,
and she never forgot how to relax,
how to allow her mind to teach,
her mind to guide,
herself to know . . .
and she changed
her way of doing things.
She returned home,
but she stayed on that vacation as well.
And you can stay relaxed,
comfortably relaxed,
as your mind drifts
in the sands of time,
and takes you there
now. . . .
[*Go to trance termination.*]

5

AFFIRMING THE SELF

The Diagnostic Trance process provides an opportunity for the unconscious mind to clarify the nature and source of a problem and to precipitate a resolution of that problem. When this permissive state of passive inner awareness fails to produce significant change, then general purpose metaphors can be used in a further effort to elicit unconscious action. If neither of these seems to yield promising results, then more straightforward therapeutic messages may be appropriate.

The examples of problem-related metaphor scripts presented in this and the following chapters are designed to offer clients a clearer view of themselves and a more straightforward understanding of potential solutions. Although these messages are directed primarily toward the unconscious mind, the metaphors are specific enough to gently challenge the conscious mind a bit as well. They plant the seeds of a specific idea or understanding which can grow from unconscious into conscious awareness.

The metaphor scripts presented in the present chapter were constructed for use with depressed, self-effacing, self-blaming clients whose underlying pain stems from critical self-evaluations coupled with recurring memories of past failures, rejections or disappointments. These scripts emphasize the correlation between such patterns of thought and subsequent feelings of depression, helplessness or worthlessness. They also stress the realization that it is up to client to change this painful, self-destructive pattern of internal events.

Many depressed clients are reluctant to change their way of thinking. They seem to cling to their misery either because they believe it is their right to feel awful given what life has done to them or because they feel that somehow it would be wrong to feel better. In the first case, the resulting behavior often seems like a justifiable temper tantrum given the client's past or present circumstances. In the second case, the client apparently has learned to feel miserable and to blame or belittle him/herself in order to protect or please someone else (often a parent). A separate script is provided for each of these cases.

THE WRECK

A metaphor about depression with underlying anger.

And so, as you know, how we feel
about something imagined or real
is really up to us.
Like the man I've heard about
who bought a new car,
a fancy sports car,
that he waxed and polished and cleaned,
at least once a week, sometimes more.
He was so proud of that car,
until one day
somebody backed into it,
put a big dent in it,
a big scrape along the side,
and he was so hurt and upset,
that he flew into a rage at first,
refused to drive it for a week,
and when he finally did drive it,
he drove it hard and fast,
and he refused to wash it or wax it,
and everytime he saw that dent,
a big depression along the side,
he became very sad and angry,
and sometimes he even cried.
It changed his whole life,
nothing made him happy anymore,
nothing seemed like fun.
He kept looking at that dent,
which reminded him how bad he felt,
how mad and upset he was.
Everytime he saw it,
he felt a twinge inside,
and he thought to himself,
"Why bother?" "Why me?"
"Nothing ever goes right anyway."
That scraped up dent began to rust
and became an ugly hole
that he glanced at every day
and felt that sad, mad feeling again.
And after a while,
he didn't want to go anywhere,

he didn't want to do anything,
because each time he went out,
he saw that hole again
and he felt bad again,
and just wanted to go inside and hide.
It was like he wanted to feel bad,
felt like he had a right to,
and he was right
but he could have done something,
because he did have insurance
unlike the people who live next to rivers
in the flood plains
where everything washes away
whenever the river rises above its banks
and they lose everything they have
but move back when the water recedes
telling reporters they are just glad to be
        alive.
I guess it is hard to be mad at a river
or to take a flood personally.
They call it an act of God
and continue to go to church
where they pray it won't happen again,
but know that it probably will
because rivers flood,
like people make mistakes or do things wrong.
It's just their nature, the way they are
and nobody thinks a river should be different
or gets angry or hurt when it does what it
        does,
and nobody worries that they caused the
        rain,
the rain that caused the flood.
They just move back in
and get on with their lives
and go swimming or boating,
glad that the sun is back,
the damage undone.
[*Go to a direct suggestion or to trance
termination.*]

ROYAL SERVICE

A metaphor about depression prompted by efforts to please or protect others.

Now, some people get a lot of pleasure
taking care of others in different ways.
Even tiny children,
who need to be taken care of themselves,
seem to genuinely enjoy doing little things
for those they love, those they care about,
those they want to protect.
I know about a young boy, Michael,
who found a baby rabbit in his yard,
its mother had been hit by a car.
So he brought it indoors to his room
and he made a soft warm bed for it,
and he went to the library
and read about taking care of it,
and he bought a tiny bottle to feed it
with the money he had saved from his
    allowance.
He fed it every four hours,
even set his alarm clock
and got up to feed it at night.
He was so happy as it grew,
and he spoke to it in those gentle tones.
It would have all been perfect
if it hadn't run away,
after it grew
the way most baby rabbits do.
So he cried when it left
but his parents made sure he knew
that it wasn't his fault,
that he'd done everything there was to do,
and they were very proud of him,
which may be why he still rescues baby
    animals
and raises them to be set free,
and seems to feel better about himself
as a result.
But that's a very different experience
from the little girl raised by a self-styled
    queen
who forbade her daughter from being better
    than her

and made sure she said she wasn't.
That little girl was raised in splendor,
pampered and spoiled in a lot of ways,
but she was never allowed to know
that she was prettier or nicer, or smarter,
or more talented than her mother ever had
    been.
And somehow that little girl knew
that she had to do whatever she could
to protect her mother from the truth.
It wasn't just that it was dangerous in those
    days
to offend the queen and make her mad,
the little girl really wanted to take care of
    her
and make sure she never got sad.
So she acted stupid and silly,
and she put on lots of weight,
and whenever she did something well,
she explained to everyone why it didn't
    count.
Little Linda became very good at one thing;
at criticizing herself and what she did,
but try as she might she still excelled
and accomplished great things in spite of
    herself,
which made it harder not to feel
like she'd done something wrong,
even years after her mother died
because there was something deep inside
which said it was bad and mean
to be better than mother in any way.
And she continued to feel that way
until one day when she finally got mad,
after sitting in a trance for a while,
and realized what her mother had done,
and decided she had a right
to take care of herself
as well as she had taken care of others.
So she learned how to praise herself,
to speak to herself in those gentle tones

and to be happy about what she was able to
    do,
and when she crawled into her soft warm
    bed,
she was able to allow herself
to feel glad to be herself
and to tell her mother she was sorry
that she had grown up to be
so content with her life and herself,
but that now it was time to be set free.
[*Go to a direct suggestion or to trance
termination.*]

THE HEARING TEST

A metaphor for low self-esteem.

And what about Beethoven,
who became increasingly deaf
as he got older,
but kept on working, writing music
that he could not hear.
Until one day, one evening,
he conducted the symphony
as they played his newest work,
a concerto.
And when it was finished
the crowd erupted in applause.
They stood and cheered,
but he could not hear.
He stood there facing the orchestra,
unaware of the audience's approval
until someone walked out
and turned him around
so he could see what he could not hear.
Only then did he know
what everyone needs to know
but sometimes cannot hear,
like the woman I have heard of,
black hair, black eyes, stocky build,
a bright professional woman
who hated herself
and hated her life.
She thought she was ugly and awful,
and she thought that was why
so many awful things had happened to her.
But one day
she was having lunch with a friend,
an artist she had known for a time,
and she said to her friend
that there were so many beautiful women
and they all seemed to be on that street that
     day,
and her friend simply said,
"I think you're the most beautiful woman
I've ever seen,"
and went on eating, as if it were nothing.

And that simple observation,
that simple statement of opinion,
matter-of-fact not flattery,
wouldn't go away,
couldn't be undone.
Her friend was an artist
who knew what beauty was,
so she could not ignore it,
and she could not forget it.
Instead she began to look at herself,
each day in the mirror
and she began to look at others,
how they looked, who they were with,
and it was very hard and scary at first
to realize how wrong she had been,
how wrong her mother had been,
how wrong she had been about herself
in so many different ways.
But over time she began to accept it,
she was not ugly,
she was not stupid,
she was not a bad person,
she was attractive and likeable and nice,
and she did not have to settle
for less than she deserved.
How she thought changed,
how she felt changed,
what she did changed,
her life changed,
all because of one brief comment,
one brief glimpse of herself,
a clear admission of something
she had been unable
to let herself know before,
that truth is beauty
and beauty truth,
and the truth about oneself, one's beauty,
is in the eye of the beholder.
But what we hear
is not always measured on a hearing test.

Beethoven heard things in his mind
that his ears could no longer hear,
and many animals can hear sounds,
that the human ear cannot,
and all we ever need to hear
is that there is nothing else we need to do,
except hear the beauty of what is.
[*Go to a direct suggestion or to trance
termination.*]

6

—

ALLEVIATING UNWARRANTED FEARS

The metaphor scripts presented in this chapter deal with the production, experience and removal of fear. They were designed to help people unconsciously learn how to prevent the thoughts or images that are triggering their anxiety and to replace them with more comfortable and useful patterns of response. Whenever a Diagnostic Trance or your own clinical insight suggests that an unwarranted fear is somehow connected to the anticipation or expectation of a catastrophic outcome, metaphors such as those presented in this chapter may be helpful.

A QUIET BIRTH

A metaphor for use with general anxiety and panic attacks.

It has been suggested,
by a French physician,
that when babies are born,
they should *not* be held upside down,
in a cold, bright, noisy operating room,
and spanked to make them cry.
Instead, they should be born
into a warm, quiet room
with soft, gentle lights
and put into a warm bath,
because when they are treated that way,
they open their eyes and look around.
They seem amazed and happy,
they even seem to smile.
They lie there quietly relaxed,
and they grow up to be happier
and more secure
all because they were treated gently,
protected and taken care of,
not hurt or scared,
but just allowed to be safe and quiet for
     a while.
A natural way of doing things
that seems to work out well,
because almost all animals
have their babies on warm spring nights
when it is safe to be born
and the mother can take care of them
and help them get used to things,
slowly and comfortably adjust to things,
and learn how to keep things
under control.
They learn to hide quietly in the tall grass,
how to remain very still,
even when there is danger near,
and they learn to play happily,
secure in the awareness
that someone is nearby, protecting them,
calmly watching out for them.
And as they get older and wiser,
they seem to calm down themselves,
and become more quiet inside and out,
as they use everything they've learned.
Because even a brief moment
can provide a lesson to be used
to keep oneself calm and quiet inside,
the way warm water can seep throughout,
even though only a small corner
rests gently in that warm bath
where a newborn child rests and smiles,
with a warm glow of safe comfort.
[*Go to a direct suggestion or trance
termination.*]

FORTUNE TELLING

A metaphor about phobias.

Because the unconscious mind
is interesting to observe
as you drift down into that trance,
where those unconscious thoughts, images
    and ideas
flash through the mind so rapidly,
like schools of fish
darting through the clear blue ocean,
startling as they suddenly appear,
their strange forms and shapes,
and then disappear, replaced by others.
Some thoughts are about the past,
others about the present or even the future,
wondering what might happen then,
what might come of what is going on,
like the frightened fortune tellers,
always seeing the end of the world
written in tea leaves and palm prints,
all the signs everywhere of doom and
    disaster.
And what to make of the fact
that if you look at the horoscopes in the
    paper,
they always suggest wealth and success,
prosperity and potentials at every turn.
While the doomsayers walk the streets
with handprinted signs
announcing the end of the world,
those who get paid and paid attention to
have a different point of view.
But at least their messages are easy to see,
not like subliminal images or words
that could be hidden in movies or TV,
telling us to be afraid of this or that,
reminding us to be concerned
that something awful is about to happen,
something awful or terrible.
Like the shape of a hawk circling above,
a shape that scares all birds
from the time they are born.

They do not have to learn to be afraid,
nature does that for them,
to protect them from real danger.
Some buildings have a cutout of that shape
pasted on large windows,
to keep birds from flying into them
and hurting themselves.
That shape scares them away,
and it cannot be unlearned,
but some things can be unlearned.
We know you won't fall off the edge of the
    world
when you sail out to sea,
and we know tomatoes are not poisonous,
and toads cannot create warts,
or that just believing we can fly,
doesn't make it so,
even though Peter Pan and Tinkerbell
can still be fun to watch,
like anything can be fun or not,
and any knot can be undone, untied,
as the unconscious mind
finds its own way
to unlearn for you
and see things in a different light,
a warm comfortable light
that allows a feeling to change,
to rearrange those thoughts and images,
to change that feeling,
like the fortune tellers said,
allowing the mind to foresee
that change in the future,
and to enjoy noticing that future change
    occur.
[*Go to a direct suggestion or to trance
termination.*]

FAIL SAFE

A metaphor for test anxiety and fear of failure.

Because everyone needs to relax at times,
even Olympic athletes
who are under a great deal of pressure to
    perform,
and sometimes must be perfect to win,
need some way to relax
and to put things into perspective,
to recognize that it is just a sport
and not a war between nations.
Because a war is one thing
and a game is something else entirely,
especially in this atomic age
where a war could mean the end of
    everything.
We really cannot afford to make
even the smallest of mistakes,
and so some people are terrified
that the fail-safe system will fail,
and that will be the end of it all,
all because of some tiny little error,
somebody doing something wrong
or saying the wrong thing at the wrong time
in the wrong way to the wrong person,
and everything goes up in flames.
Which is why they have special programs,
for the people working with those systems,
because what they have to do
is so dangerous and so terribly important
that special training and counseling is
    required.
The only place in the world, perhaps,
where mistakes cannot be allowed,
and it is comforting to note
that almost everyplace else,
an error is just an opportunity
to do it differently later on,
because perfection is rarely required
and perfection is seldom needed,
and even Olympic athletes,
are never perfect all the time,

and sometimes do things wrong
like the Navahos when they weave a rug,
who always leave a knot, an imperfection,
so the gods won't be angered
and think they are trying to be gods
    themselves.
But that is another story
about what is really important
and what is not
and how it feels to give permission
to enjoy the feeling of the freedom
to feel safe doing those things
knowing that the world won't end,
if you leave a knot someplace,
so the gods can relax
knowing you are not challenging them,
just doing the best you can,
letting it go at that.
[*Go to a direct suggestion or to trance
termination.*]

BREAKDOWNS

A metaphor for cardiac neuroses.

When something is really valuable,
people get afraid of losing it,
Like the man who bought
a new Cadillac car.
It was his life's dream,
he had wanted one his whole life
and he put his life savings into it.
He felt proud to own such a beautiful
      machine,
and he was excited when he drove it home.
All his life he had heard what great cars
      they were,
so reliable and well built,
so safe and dependable.
He loved the way it sounded when he closed
      the doors,
everything seemed to work so smoothly and
      well.
Even though it was used
it seemed to be in perfect condition,
so it never occurred to him
that something might go wrong
until one day that week he and his wife went
      for a drive,
and when they were miles out into the
      country
a hose to the radiator broke,
the car overheated,
and there they were, stranded, frightened,
      angry,
waiting for a tow truck from the dealer to
      rescue them.
And when they finally got home
he parked that car in the garage
and he refused to go on any more long
      drives.
He drove it to work at times,
but he was always listening, waiting
for something else to go wrong.
His wife told him he was being silly,

but it didn't feel silly to him.
He felt betrayed and disappointed
and his dreams of driving on long vacations,
exploring places they never had been,
all turned into thoughts of being stranded
      again,
of being someplace where no one could fix it,
as if the local dealer
were the only one who knew anything about
      his car.
So his wife took that car to a mechanic
and had him go over it with a fine toothed
      comb.
He replaced everything worn or weathered,
he tuned the engine and changed the plugs,
he put extra belts and hoses in the trunk
and he test drove it over old back roads,
and then they went home and got her
      husband
and took him for a drive in the country,
and the mechanic told him everything he
      had done,
and reassured him that his car
was in excellent shape for its age
but that it needed to be driven on long
      drives
to keep the engine cleaned out
which gave his wife a perfect excuse
to plan a vacation for the next month.
Before they left on their two thousand mile
      drive,
he bought a CB and a cellular phone,
so that no matter where they were
they could always get help if something
      went wrong,
and he still was very concerned at first,
but when some stranger told him
what a beautiful car he had
he started to relax and feel good again,
and began to enjoy the trip.

He still checks that car over carefully each
    day,
and washes and waxes it often,
and of course a few things have gone wrong
and it has had to be worked on a few times,
but now he is retired
and his life's dream belongs to him
and he can enjoy it comfortably,
feeling safe and secure and proud.
[*Go to a direct suggestion or to trance
termination.*]

7

UNDOING BAD
TRANCES

An underlying assumption of the following scripts is that the various alterations in perception manifested by somatoform and dissociative disorders frequently represent a self-protective misuse of various self-hypnotic abilities. Hence, the metaphors presented in this chapter are designed to imply that there may be better ways to protect the individual, that such protection may no longer be necessary, or that the symptoms themselves are impressive demonstrations of hypnotic abilities which may have more practical uses. It should be obvious that the metaphors for recovery from trauma presented in Chapter 8 may also be relevant to the clients experiencing dissociative reactions.

MERGING

A metaphor for multiple personality disorders.

And while you drift,
the mind drifts,
like water from one place to another,
automatically, effortlessly flowing,
going the easiest way
down toward the sea.
And when you fly above it,
you see the paths it takes,
the tiny creeks and streams,
that wind their way down the hills,
down to the valleys below
where they flow into the river,
and that river flows along,
getting larger and larger,
gaining more and more
from each new stream that joins it.
And those rivers flow together,
a larger river forms,
and it flows too,
it flows gently but surely toward the sea.
It winds its way around mountains,
it surges through the plains,
gathering more and more strength,
from other streams and rivers along the
        way,
and eventually it reaches the bay,
where it spreads throughout the delta
and joins the power of the ocean,
and becomes a part of that sea of life,
a part of everything.
And while you continue to relax,
I would like to talk to all of you,
to all the you's there are,
because a bunch of yews together
can be a marvelous forest,
and one yew alone
is just a tree in the middle of nowhere.
When things join together
they gain strength and protection
from each other.

It is a sign of the times,
headlines in the newspaper each day
describe the way small companies
are forming large healthy companies
by joining together,
a merger of resources.
Several small banks
announced a merger the other day
and it was difficult
to work out who would be in charge,
but eventually they worked it out
so that everyone was happy,
everyone was represented,
and each group had its say
so that in a short time,
when they change all the signs,
and they change all the labels,
no one will ever know
that things weren't always that way.
It will just seem to be
the way it's supposed to be
to be together as one,
to be one,
like a special color
that is several colors
blended together
to be a new color,
a special color
all its own
in that painting
a portrait perhaps of a family,
a group of people living as one,
where each has special abilities,
and each has a special purpose to serve,
but sometimes they begin to keep secrets,
from each other and from the world,
and when that happens
they are brought together
and told to tell each other
those secrets they all need to know.

Because when mother has a secret
or father has a secret
or brother or sister have secrets,
and they have secrets from outsiders,
the family begins to fall apart,
and each member loses something,
because they all need each other,
and they all need to be loved by each other,
but secrets keep them from each other,
and they begin to be mean to each other,
when they need to tell each other
they are very, very sorry
and they need to come together
to cry together, to love together,
to share their lives and strengths
so that when they have their portrait
      painted,
they look like they belong together as one,
and the artist can merge the colors
as the relief and relaxation of them all,
allows the minds to drift together
winding gently but surely toward the sea,
where each can see and feel
that secure feeling of belonging,
here and now, safe and sound,
because things change
as relaxation occurs,
and an openness provides
a well-deserved rest
after the effort it took
to overcome those problems
and to join together
as one.
[*Go to a direct suggestion or to trance
termination.*]

AMPLIFIERS

A metaphor about somatoform disorders.

And so, as you listen to me,
you can notice that sometimes
my voice may seem louder than others,
or other sounds may become apparent,
because the mind can magnify anything
or change our awareness of some things
the way tiny electrical circuits
can be used to amplify sound.
Tiny little microchips
you can barely see on the end of your finger
now are used every day
to make little sounds louder
or to change music into flashing lights,
so that it has become harder to ignore
what otherwise might have gone overlooked.
They can even use highly sensitive
    instruments
to hear the sounds given off by trees
as they dry out during a drought,
and have found that those sounds
seem to attract insects,
which then attack those weakened trees,
that now have very little resistance
and are unable to fight off those bugs,
which are very different bugs
from the kind that are used by spies
to overhear secret conversations
or to catch people in private lies.
They also amplify sounds
most of us would ignore,
because if we could hear everything,
it would be too noisy to hear anything,
and all we would hear would be a roar.
The roar of squeaks and creaks and thumps,
of tiny squeals and bumps and cracks
that everything lets out
everytime it moves
or changes temperature
or changes position.
Even the human body

produces many more noises than we hear,
because the ear can't hear it all
and the brain decides that most of it
isn't worth paying attention to.
Even the conversation next door
usually is ignored
once we decide
that it is safe to do so,
we can ignore anything at all
that really is not important,
but how do you build a computer
that can decide what is important
and what is not,
and do so wisely and correctly
so that each noise that means nothing
is left behind
and only those things are amplified
which are worth hearing.
That would be an invention worth having,
and using every day.
[*Go to a direct suggestion or to trance
termination.*]

LOSING THINGS

A metaphor about dissociative and somatoform disorders.

We all have so many abilities,
and we can use those abilities
in so many different ways.
We can learn to forget a promise,
and not have to go to that party after all,
even though we meant to, we forgot,
and everybody knows
that forgetting occurs.
Or we can lose an object,
keys perhaps, or an important book,
and no matter how hard we look,
no matter how much we search,
that object stays lost,
put away where we put it
for safekeeping
or just to get it out of the way.
But how about those rare souls,
who refuse to use what they have.
Aunt Bessy was very old-fashioned,
she was very set in her ways,
she really believed it was wrong
to rely upon new-fangled inventions.
So she heated her curling iron on the stove,
and she had a water pump out back,
and to keep the lights turned off,
she went to bed when it was dark.
Her house was cold and stark,
until her later years,
when suddenly she sold her place
and moved into a retirement village,
a place her church ran,
where she began to use a TV,
and electric lights, and an electric iron,
and she seemed to be so much happier,
a happiness many children feel
when left alone and allowed to be themselves.
A child in a scary movie,
closes his eyes and covers his ears,
then in later years just watches,
unconcerned and unafraid,

at least that's what's happened,
to everybody I know,
though not everybody I know
has the ability to do
what a simple reptile can do.
Like the glass-tailed lizard,
that simply loses its tail
whenever something grabs it,
and leaves it there behind,
distracting everything
while it runs away and hides,
because every living thing
has some way to protect itself,
and the mother quail protects its young . . .
she pretends to be injured,
and runs away from the nest,
distracting dangerous predators,
the way a magician distracts attention
from the real issue,
so that now you see it,
now you don't,
an illusion of disappearance
brought on to keep the mind
from seeing what really happened,
though a child could see the reality
because children do not know
what not to pay attention to,
and they see clearly the trick,
except when blinded by the light
as they leave the movies during the day,
though they recover their sight
and find it difficult to forget
what they know they have seen.
So they recover quickly
what only seemed to be lost
and so can you,
as your unconscious mind,
let's you know what you know,
so you can do what you can do,
in the right way for you,

slowly or quickly,
able to pay attention to
what otherwise would go overlooked
in order to ignore or not know
what your unconscious mind knows
and protects you from now
until you're ready to know
and it knows that you are ready,
ready to find that lost object,
the keys to that book,
a storybook that tells a tale,
a story worth knowing.
[*Go to a direct suggestion or to trance
termination.*]

BANISHMENT

A metaphor about somatoform and dissociative disorders.

So while you relax
and the mind drifts in dreams,
I can remind you
of something you may never have seen,
or read, or even heard about,
though it was written about,
and a movie was made,
called The Liar in Winter,
no, The Lion in Winter,
the story of a king,
his bride, Eleanor of Aquitaine,
a passionate romance
between a king and a queen.
He locked her in a tower,
banished her from his kingdom,
only let her out on holidays,
because she was so rebellious,
a quality he desired
but feared at the same time.
Rebellion against the rules of the time
gave him a freedom of passion with her
but her rebellion threatened him too
with the loss of his kingly rule,
so he banished her,
refused to see her
except now and then,
and they lived their lives in torment
married but separate
from what they wanted,
what they needed,
afraid that each would destroy the other,
until both had little left to lose.
Only then did they come together,
and accept how much they had lost,
while trying not to lose control.
Because control is an issue even for a little
        child.
Daniel was his name,
and he always seemed to get sick
whenever there was something

he did not want to do.
He wanted to control what happened,
to control what he had to do,
and this little four-year-old boy
was able to be in charge
because his unconscious mind
somehow knew how to do that,
it knew how to make him sick
when there was something
he did not want to face.
It also knew how to forget,
and how to remember things to him too.
Thoughts, ideas, images perhaps
would suddenly spring into his mind,
sometimes in that drifting quiet time
when the body is relaxed
and the mind drifts free,
he would suddenly see,
in his mind's eye
the answer to some problem or question.
The solution would just appear
just like the temperature of his non-sickness,
a gift from the unconscious.
But what to do
when you get someone a gift,
and later you realize
that that gift was not right for them?
Perhaps it was too tight,
or the wrong style or color
or something not really needed,
not the best way to do something,
and so you take it back,
you exchange it,
you get something else instead,
or you just get the cost back,
and wait until later
when a better idea
pops into your head,
a thought, a memory, an understanding,
that makes it all

so much easier than before.
That's right,
easier than banishing a loved one
into the darkest depths of the night.
But then, that's another story
isn't it.
[*Go to a direct suggestion or to trance
termination.*]

8

—

RECOVERING FROM TRAUMA

Some people are haunted by vague or clear memories of excruciatingly painful events. The memories may be vague and elusive or quite clear and the events may be recent or long past, but their impact upon the person's life is ever present. Nothing can ever undo what happened in the past, but there may be a way to undo what the past is doing to a client in the present.

Healing the effects of a past trauma is neither simple nor easy. Sometimes it involves the development of a new perspective on what happened in order to remove all blame from the victim, to direct the anger outward, and to empower the person in the future. At other times, it involves an acknowledgment of the futility of trying to understand or change what happened, along with a mournful letting go of that past. Almost invariably, however, recovery from trauma involves the reestablishment of some precious inner resource that the traumatic event tore away from the client. Child sexual abuse often shatters the feeling of one's innocent goodness. Physical abuse can destroy the awareness of personal self-worth. Loss of a loved one can disconnect the person from the ability to love. The damage done varies from client to client but the therapeutic goal remains the same: to help that client recover what was lost and to prevent further suffering.

The pain such people experience can be more devastating than any other form of pain imaginable. Because their initial trauma was so intense and thorough, the subsequent suffering experienced may continue at an unconscious level long after an apparent conscious resolution of the issues involved. For this reason, metaphorical hypnotherapeutic interventions, such as those presented below, can be of considerable value. We do not want to imply that these techniques can be relied upon exclusively to resolve such problems. They are, however, an effective adjunct to the many forms of support and intervention specifically tailored to the needs of survivors of assault and those in the mourning process.

LITTLE DREAMS

A metaphor for adult survivors of child sexual assault.

Now, you've told me many things about your
    life
and listening to the truth about someone's
    life
is a privilege and an honor . . .
and though you don't need my thanks
I really do thank your conscious mind
for sorting and categorizing so much
    information
and I thank your unconscious mind
for what you can let your conscious mind
    discover
later on.
And there are so many things
a person can discover.
I remember the time,
five or six years ago
when I first discovered what it would be like
to live an entire life
feeling different every day
because that's when I met Annie
and she was the only dwarf I'd ever met.
And I learned that in childhood
it really hadn't been a problem
'cause everyone was small and little then,
but friends grew up
and Annie stayed small,
and had to go on living her life
in a world of big people.
She had a special stool in the kitchen,
she pushed it around as she moved
from counter, to cabinet,
so she could jump on top of it
and reach out for the things she needed,
so she could look into the freezer,
and reach the burners on the stove.
She had a special sewing machine
and she made all her own clothes
from her own designs
since nothing else would fit.

At a party she couldn't reach the punch
    bowl,
and she sometimes had to crawl onto a chair
where her feet never touched ground.
And I really wanted to learn from her
about living such a life,
and she told me,
"There's just one thing you can say about
    people like me,
there's always going to be something that
    comes up."
And I thought a long time about that
and what it might mean in a life.
Now a client I worked with a while back
told me about a dream he'd had
where he'd awakened in his bedroom,
but the entire room was covered with a
    dense fog.
And when he first felt the fog he was quite
    angry,
finding himself damp and uncomfortable
and unable to see a foot ahead of him,
and the anger just grew and grew
until he felt nothing but rage,
and that heavy fog enveloping him.
He wanted to run screaming from the room,
but when he opened his mouth to speak
nothing came out,
and who would he tell?
He was so alone.
And how could there be so much fog?
Would anyone believe him?
And these thoughts occupied his mind,
he couldn't move, he couldn't cry,
he could only feel his anger,
rusting like a nail in the dense fog.
And just when things seemed darkest
he became aware of a breath of warm air
hovering around his face.
And you can imagine his surprise

to discover that that warm, moist air
was his own breath mingling with the fog.
And he continued to breathe
deep, strong breaths, blowing that fog away
with every inhalation and exhalation
as the fog lifted
and light began filtering into that room,
anger lifting, breathing calmly, peacefully,
and he awakened from that dream
with a new understanding.
And it was about the same time
that his sister received the letter
about the inheritance.
Now he and his sister were orphaned
at a very early age,
and they had impressed upon me
that their expectations from childhood
didn't include having anyone look out for
     them,
or take care of them.
They were all alone in the world,
on their own in the world,
or so it seemed to them,
until the day they got the letter telling them
they were to receive a large inheritance.
And their puzzlement grew and grew,
since they were orphans, alone in the world.
But adults so often forget the things
they knew so well as children,
just as they'd forgotten the times
they'd saved a penny here, a nickel there,
and left them for safekeeping
with a kind, old woman up the street,
who'd taken their money and invested it
with her own
until she could return
their own savings to them
multiplied into the thousands and thousands.
And with so many resources to rely on,
a child, robbed of a parent,
became rich as an adult,
safe, and comforted now.
And though you sometimes dream in
     darkness,

that is one of your lives by now—
it is not the time that you know best,
so much of the journey
has been in shadow . . .
now you are safe
you know life in light,
where there is no pressure, no rush to
     change,
only the time without shadows.
[*Go to a direct suggestion or to trance
termination.*]

SAYING GOODBYE

A metaphor for adult survivors of abusive childhoods, child abuse, and trauma.

Now,
as you sit there with your eyes closed,
and begin to continue to allow your body to
relax,
your mind to relax,
and experience the awareness of many
different things,
you may begin to wonder,
how many different ways there are
to heal a wound,
a wound from long ago that never healed
but remained behind
to change the way you think and feel,
like a woman I know who always wondered
why
she was the way she was,
until one day she discovered a child within—
a sad child, an unhappy child,
an angry hurt child from long ago.
A child she always heard in the background,
a child she protected and did everything for
today,
a child who made her feel so sad
and she would do anything to keep that child
quiet,
to keep that child happy,
to give that child what it wanted and needed.
And I asked her what needed to be done,
and she said she needed to say *goodbye* to
that child,
she needed to *hug* that child,
to *hold* that child
and to *tell* that child how very, very,
sorry she was
that those things had happened to it.
She felt so badly for the pain,
so badly for the fear,
so badly for the anger.
But she knew she had to say goodbye,
finally,

she had to leave it behind
and go on with her life.
She knew there was nothing she could do
to save that child,
to change the past,
to undo what was.
What was, was and there was nothing she
could do.
So she hugged that child, and said goodbye,
and walked away, and cried and cried.
The hardest thing she had ever done
was say goodbye, leave it behind,
abandon it to the past.
She felt awful, but she knew
that was what she had to do.
There was nothing she could do to change
the past,
nothing she could do to undo
what that child went through.
But afterwards she was free,
felt free, to do what *she* wanted.
The child was gone
and she was free,
free of the past,
free to be.
And so as you relax,
and continue to drift down,
your unconscious knows what you can do,
your conscious knows it too,
and you can feel the freedom
of that relaxed letting go
in your own way,
even as you drift more deeply at times than
others.
[*Go to trance termination.*]
[*A modified version of this procedure was
submitted to the American Society of Clinical
Hypnosis for inclusion in the ASCH Handbook,
edited by D. Corydon Hammon, Ph.D.*]

BURIED TREASURES

A metaphor for those who have lost someone or some part of themselves.

I wonder if you have ever seen
the small fragile glass figurines
that artisans sell at fairs and in shopping
    malls,
made of tiny strands of clear bright glass
all carefully laced together
to form the shape of a ship or an animal,
or even a house or a tree,
that seem to fascinate children
with their delicate sparkles and shapes
like priceless jewels, valuable possessions,
to be carried in velvet cases and protected,
kept safe from loss or damage,
tiny treasures, a gift to someone,
like the treasure carried in ships across the
    sea.
There was a program on TV several years
    ago,
about a man who spent twenty years
searching for such a ship, a lost treasure
    ship,
one of hundreds that had been lost along the
    coast
because of accidents and disasters and wars.
He researched it very carefully,
and thought he knew exactly what had been
    lost.
He also thought he knew what had
    happened
and where the treasure had sunk.
But it was hard to find that ship,
it had been lost for so long.
It had gotten buried with mud and coral,
and there were many other wrecks in the
    area,
any one of which could have been the one,
but wasn't.
So he spent many years searching,
and he raised thousands of dollars from
    investors,
because he was convinced

there was something of great value down
    there,
lost treasure of immeasurable worth,
and he convinced others it was there too,
family, friends and the divers who worked
    with him,
searched for it year after year,
until finally one day
the divers returned to the surface
shouting and screaming and holding up gold
    bars.
They had found that ship,
and it contained more than you can imagine,
tons of gold bars, silver bars, gold coins,
precious jewels and elaborate jewelry,
priceless objects, treasure untold,
things from the past that had gone untouched,
that had not been seen for hundreds of years
suddenly were there for people to hold and
    to feel.
And they held them with reverence,
touching them gently and silently,
as if these things that had been lost for so
    long,
contained some memory of the past,
something special that people need,
something special to protect,
like those tiny glass figures
that you see at fairs and malls.
They seem to be so fragile,
so easily broken by someone rough,
but they actually are quite sturdy
and can survive for years and years,
even when lost or hidden away,
like the treasures at the bottom of the
    ocean,
hidden deep down below,
something precious and valuable inside,
a part of you, before,
that belonged to you, before.
And the joy of its discovery,

the recovery of that buried treasure,
the pleasure of knowing it belongs to you,
something you can bring back with you
that warm good part of the heart of the
     matter
that children sometimes lose for a time,
or have taken from them at another time,
but it always lies there waiting,
waiting to be brought back to the surface
where it can be touched and protected and
     enjoyed
and kept close with you forever, now,
because it all belongs to you.
[*Go to a direct suggestion or to trance
termination.*]

9

———

DEVELOPING SPONTANEITY

Often clients need to learn how to stop trying to do something that would occur naturally if they simply allowed it to do so. In essence, this involves learning how to trust the unconscious and how to turn off all of the self-talk that blocks or prevents the spontaneous occurrence of the desired response. The metaphors contained in the scripts in this chapter are designed to embed this trust and to establish alternative reactions.

LEARNING TO RIDE

A metaphor for sexual dysfunction.

There are many different ways
to do what you want to do,
but there is only one way
to let it be done for you,
because there are many things
we don't know how to do
and so we can learn to trust
and allow them to be done.
They will be done
when you allow them to
like learning to ride a horse.
At first it can be difficult
to just relax and ride,
but the horse
has its own rhythm
and its own power
and once you find that rhythm
and relax into it,
that horse will carry you
wherever you want to go.
Like your own unconscious mind,
it has the power and ability
to do those things automatically,
though at first
it can be rather scary,
and you may hold on tight,
worried about every move,
every thing that happens . . .
wondering if it is supposed to be that way
or if that horse can be trusted.
But after a while you learn . . .
how to relax
and enjoy those things that occur
quite automatically,
that effortless movement,
that automatic flow . . .
and the mind relaxes,
drifting off someplace else entirely,
enjoying thoughts or images,
like riding a tour bus,
looking out the window,
enjoying the scenes and sights,
knowing the driver knows
where to go and when,
knowing it is safe to just watch,
or to drift off in dreams,
a dream of joining the circus perhaps,
to walk a tightrope,
which looks harder than it is,
and only is hard because it is so high,
so high you begin to worry and try
and trying to do it
makes it hard to do,
but doing it without thinking,
allowing the unconscious to take over,
makes it easier and easier.
Just like typing or playing the piano,
where the fingers skip over the keys
in an effortless flow of rhythm
until someone asks which finger
you use for F or P.
The body knows,
but you don't know,
and so doing what you want to do
is just going along for the ride,
letting it be done to you,
as your unconscious mind
allows you to forget to remember
to try to do what you cannot do,
because you can forget,
or your unconscious mind can forget
to remember it to you.
So that in a short time,
you can just relax
absorbed by the sights and sounds
of your own mind's eye
while that horse continues on
and you ride without knowing it,
anywhere at all.
[*Go to a direct suggestion or to trance
termination.*]

BEAUTIFUL GIFTS

A metaphor about premature ejaculation.

The unconscious mind guards a variety of
    treasures,
like a guard in an art museum,
standing in a room full of sculptures
and paintings of beautiful women.
They get to observe the reactions
of people as they walk into that room,
and hear the sudden exclamations,
the "Oohs" and "Aahs" of appreciation
that just burst forth from their lips
as soon as they see those things
that are so beautiful it takes the breath
    away.
It is easy to demonstrate our appreciation
with that unexpected, uncontrolled response,
the same kind of reaction you see in children
when they receive a special gift, a toy
    perhaps,
a birthday present or a Christmas present.
It can be fun to watch their uncontrolled
    excitement
as they tear off the wrapping paper
and throw it everywhere
and jerk out that toy
and start playing with it at once
and probably break it
before they even have a chance to say
    "Thank you!"
But it can be more satisfying
watching an adult receive a gift,
carefully examining the package,
appreciating the beauty of the wrapping,
and slowly undoing it,
savoring each moment of anticipation,
enjoying the pleasure of each step,
stretching it out over time,
not giving in to the temptations,
but taking their time to enjoy each step,
pausing every now and then to say something,
to express their appreciation,
wondering out loud what it could be,
and then finally opening the box,
taking out the gift slowly, gently,
softly expressing their pleasure
in a deep and genuine way,
letting the giver receive attention for a
    time,
telling them how wonderful and thoughtful.
And then, and only then,
when everything else has been done,
finally exploring the present completely,
enjoying themselves thoroughly,
like real art lovers
who also take their time,
they allow the beauty to sink in,
they sit and ponder and enjoy each one
for hours and hours on end.
With a quiet reverence and respect
they pay tribute in a quiet way,
that takes them far away
from the crowds of noisy children
skipping through yelling "Look at this and
    that."
And through it all
the guard stands back
watching and protecting,
knowing that sometimes a teacher comes in,
calms the children, gets their attention
and slowly and carefully explains to them
how to look at the beauty quietly,
how to see what's really there,
so that they too can sit and stare
and feel the pleasure grow
as they slowly begin to know
how to control their own awareness.
[*Go to a direct suggestion or to trance
termination.*]

LOOKING

A metaphor for impotence and anorgasmia.

They say a watched pot never boils
but the truth is
it is heat that makes the water boil
and all the watching in the world
can't stop that bubbling
once the pot reaches 212 degrees.
Waiting and watching only makes it seem
like forever, like it will never happen,
but a good cook knows
that once you start the fire
and put the pot on
then all you need to do,
is peel the carrots and onions or thaw the
        peas
or eat a few to enjoy yourself
while you wait happily for what is bound to
        happen,
as that heat continues to rise and rise
to the boiling point.
But some people still are afraid to watch,
to pay close attention as the steam rises,
and the first bubbles begin to form.
They seem to believe
they should not pay attention to such
        things,
even though sometimes you have to watch,
you have to participate fully
if you really want it to be a success,
so you can add things to the pot
when the temperature is just right
or pull them out when they are done.
And you have to pay close attention
to get a feel for cooking that way,
the way you do
when you want to examine the texture of
        something
to see if it is smooth enough or rough.
So you close your eyes and taste it,
or focus fully on that feeling,
and even the tiniest sensation gets noticed

because you are not distracted
by anything else at all.
And everything seems magnified,
becomes the full focus of your experience,
and you can just allow those sensations to
        grow,
to become the only thing you feel
as you observe them with pleasure
and look forward to that meal.
A good cook can almost taste it in your
        mind's eye,
and when that happens
the salivary glands begin to do their thing,
and the anticipation of something delicious
makes it harder and harder
to wait any longer
until you can finally
let yourself take that first bite,
and feel the relief and satisfaction
of a job well done,
like the great gourmets of the world
who learn to appreciate
fine wines, fine food,
and all the other pleasures available to
        them.
[*Go to a direct suggestion or to trance
termination.*]

FIREMEN

A metaphor for bashful bladder syndrome.

Whenever people learn to do anything
they always seem to want to show off
to see who can do it best,
who can do it the longest
or the quickest
or the most precisely.
Even firemen,
who are trained to save lives,
get together every now and then
for contests and demonstrations
to see which team can get there fastest,
connect the hoses and hit the target first,
or who can push a ball across the line
with the most powerful stream of water
those fire engines can pump.
And spectators come from all over
to watch these strange contests
where hoses are connected to fire hydrants,
and valves are quickly opened
to release that high pressure stream
which can knock a person down
if they are not careful.
It's easy to forget
that this equipment is used to save lives,
that all that practice has a serious purpose,
so that when that moment comes
when they need to connect those hoses
and open up those valves,
they can stay relaxed
and know what to do
and not be in too big a hurry
or worry about what to do next,
because they've done it over and over
so that as soon as they arrive
they can stay calm and take charge
and do what needs to be done,
whether there is anyone watching or not
is not something worth noticing,
because they are there to do a job,
not to win or lose a contest,

not to look good or stylish,
or to worry about what the neighbors think
but just to do what they need to do
to put out that fire
and to worry about showing off later,
just like the animals in a zoo,
who seem totally unconcerned
that anyone else is there,
and just do what they do
whether in a zoo or not.
[*Go to a direct suggestion or to trance
termination.*]

DRAWING ATTENTION

A metaphor for insomnia.

Have you ever tried
to not think of a pink elephant,
to avoid thinking of a pink elephant at all
　　costs?
There is a lesson there
but it is different from the lesson learned
when you try to do something
only your unconscious can do for you,
because no one can think a thought
that will add one inch to their height
or digest their food in a different way,
and if you ever go someplace with a child
who is very, very hungry,
you will very quickly learn
that telling a child to ignore that hunger
won't help matters at all.
They know they want something
and they want it now
and telling them to ignore it
won't help to forget it
but distracting their attention
with something of great interest
may help them forget that hunger entirely.
So you can take them on a roller coaster
or you can do something that makes them
　　laugh,
or you can have them close their eyes
and draw circles on their forehead
asking them to tell you
what color is this circle,
and what color is the next,
and what color is the line you trace
from one side to the other,
that looks a bit like the edge of a pond,
with cattails growing here and there,
and rabbits playing in the grass
while the sun shines warmly
and the breeze gently blows in the trees
as the water washes against the shore
and the turtles sleep in the light

with clouds drifting by above
in the clear blue sky,
changing form and shape
as the birds sing to each other.
And that drifting off occurs
without knowing where or when
even as the child tries
to open the eyes
and to not drift away,
that pleasant scene quiets the mind
and helps it forget to try
to be aware or unaware
of anything at all,
and that's all there needs to be
and all you need to do.
[*Go to a direct suggestion or to trance
termination.*]

10

—

ENHANCING RELATIONSHIPS

When the presenting problem involves a relationship, we prefer to work with both people at the same time. This is true even if the primary source of the problem appears to be the unwarranted insecurity, jealousy or blocked emotions of only one of the two people involved. Thus, the metaphor scripts presented in this chapter are appropriate for use with couples who have participated in a trance induction together and are now ready for the therapist to clarify the situation and to offer suggestions for alternative resolutions. These metaphors also can be used with individuals seeking help because of a history of insecurity, jealousy or fear of commitment. However, we recommend that interpersonal difficulties be dealt with in an interpersonal manner, that is, with a partner, whenever this is feasible. By involving a partner in the process, it becomes possible to alter the outcome of the undesirable behavior and to break the dynamic that has supported it in the past.

For example, insecure individuals seem unable to trust themselves or the relationship. Their constant and insatiable demands for reassurance can exasperate even the most loving and comforting partner and eventually drive that person away. This outcome then further reinforces their insecurity. Similarly, jealousy tends to produce the very outcome the person is trying hardest to prevent. Suspicious efforts to control the thoughts and behavior of the partner almost invariably result in a rebellious assertion of the partner's rights to do whatever he/she wants. Finally, blocked emotional involvement or the withholding of interpersonal commitment frequently seems to be a protection against getting hurt. But by holding back emotionally the person virtually guarantees that his/her partner eventually will withdraw as well. Once again, the original concerns are confirmed in a self-fulfilling prophecy and the outcome the person is trying to prevent is exactly what occurs.

The metaphor scripts presented in this chapter convey this self-defeating, self-fulfilling prophecy quality of the behavior involved and offer each member of the relationship suggestions for an alternative approach. The goal is to break the destructive cycle and to pave the way for a meaningful, safe and rewarding relationship.

It should be noted that the phenomena of jealousy, insecurity and blocked emotional involvement often occur together in a relationship in an interactive manner. For example, blocked emotional involvement by one person may result in insecurity or jealousy from the other. Likewise, insecurity or jealousy may prompt the partner to withdraw or block further emotional involvement. Any or all of the following metaphors may apply in these situations.

It also should be noted that emotional unavailability can be the result of an addictive involvement rather than being a self-protective emotional withdrawal. When addiction to alcohol, drugs, another person or some outside activity is the reason for emotional withholding in a relationship, that addiction must be the focus of the intervention. The following scripts are not relevant to that difficulty.

TERRITORIALITY

A metaphor about jealousy.

Now, as each of both of you
continue to listen to me,
I can begin to wonder
if either or both of you,
separately or together,
have ever had the experience
of watching a dog mark out its territory.
Because dogs, and many other animals,
spend a lot of time establishing boundaries,
using scents to say this belongs to me.
Some animals have special glands
that give off a peculiar scent,
and others just urinate here and there,
and then act like that land belongs to them,
the same way countries put up fences,
and draw imaginary lines on maps,
and then say that everything here,
belongs to us for us to use anyway we want,
and everyone here has to do what we want,
        too,
whether they want to or not,
they have to do what the dictator says,
until there is a revolution
or the people move someplace else
or the dictator changes the rules
and lets the people do as they want,
lets the people make the decisions
and declare freedom throughout the land,
which requires a lot of faith and trust
that the people will do what's best,
and won't just up and leave
as soon as they have the chance.
But if that leader believes in them
and they believe in their leader,
if they respect each other and themselves,
then democracy seems to work
and people vote for who they like best,
like a popularity contest
or the way we select our favorite movie
        stars,

who may seem to be one thing,
but turn out to be another,
like the big, tough man's man
who actually is soft and gentle
or the handsome leading man
who doesn't even like women,
and what about the high school star
who shows up at the class reunion,
and turns out to be a bum,
never even had a decent job,
but he still wants to tell everybody else
what to do and how to do it,
because one of the things you learn
as a therapist
is that things sometimes are not what they
        seem.
We imagine how happy the rich folk are,
and we think we know what goes on there,
but when you really talk to people,
in private where they tell the truth,
you discover that what we imagine
is rarely accurate or even close,
and that we can imagine anything,
but that doesn't make it so,
even though we can find evidence for it,
in trashy papers and magazines.
What we really see behind the scenes
is that everyone needs something special,
and that all the boundaries dissolve,
when the dog finally lets you pet him,
and you scratch his back or behind his ears,
and play with him for a while,
he doesn't growl anymore
when you cross his urinary line,
or enter into his territory
with a bone or something sweet,
and you let him lick your hand,
and play a few games
so that later on
that friendship allows each of you

to come and go as you wish,
comfortable in the knowledge
that there is a trust in each other
you can bank on,
and that it makes good sense
and is in your best interest
to do so.
[*Go to a direct suggestion or to trance
termination.*]

PLAYGROUNDS

A metaphor for couples dealing with the issues of insecurity and trust.

Each of you has a brain,
that you use in everyday life,
that thinks, and understands and remembers,
and you depend upon it,
to provide you with the abilities needed,
to take care of things for you.
But I wonder if you know
that the neurons in that brain
can inhibit each other
or excite each other
so that when some neurons fire
they excite others,
but when other neurons fire
they inhibit the others
and keep them from responding at all.
And so there are times
when the harder those cells try
to do one thing,
the more difficult it becomes,
while at other times
not doing anything at all
gives the desired results.
And if one neuron is stimulated too much,
it may become exhausted
and stop responding completely,
just like the cells in a muscle
that get tired of doing the same thing
over and over again.
This is true even for little children,
who may be afraid at first
when their parents take them to the
        playground
and turn them loose to run around.
You can watch that tiny toddler,
unsure of itself at first,
unsure of the parent too,
afraid that parent may disappear
if it gets too far away.
So at first you go with them,
you reassure them that it is O.K.
to go off to play in the sandbox
or to explore the swings.
And that toddler keeps coming back,
but staying away longer and longer,
beginning to play with others,
even getting on the teeter totter
and learning how to balance,
each trusting the other
not to get off suddenly,
the kind of trust it takes
to invest your life's savings
in a business with a friend,
Not the kind of thing you'd do
with a total stranger,
but there are some people
who we know that we can trust
because they have earned that trust
like interest in a bank
that you count on to be there,
even though you know
that banks do fail sometimes
but it is pretty rare,
so we trust them,
unless we have a good reason not to,
just like that child trusts others.
They are all friends
unless they prove they're not,
and when that friend gets tired
of doing the same thing over and over,
they go off together
and do something else,
on the swings, or in the sandbox,
knowing their parents are there,
waiting at the picnic bench
to take them home when they're tired,
to bring them back when they're not,
and because that all goes without saying,
they can enjoy themselves
quite completely.
[*Go to a direct intervention or to trance
termination.*]

DROUGHTS

A metaphor for difficulties with emotional commitments.

There are some plants
that find it easier to survive a drought
because they have deep roots
burrowed down into the soil,
down where it stays damp and moist
even when the ground is hard and dry.
But most grasses have shallow roots,
fine roots that go down just below the
　　　surface,
so they dry out when the rains stop
and are unable to get nutrients,
the things they need to stay alive.
Because once the nutrients stop flowing in,
the growing stops as well
and the dying starts,
just like any living tissue
which is why you loosen a tourniquet
once every three or four minutes at least,
and let the blood flow through again
to nourish the cells
and to take away the wastes,
even though it may mean
that the bleeding starts again,
because we all have lots of blood
and we can stand to lose a bit,
but we can't stand to block the flow
of those things needed very long.
And the marvel of it all
is that we can donate to each other,
we can give each other what we need
and never miss it at all,
the way a plant with deep roots
can give us moisture even in a drought,
while shallow rooted grass
becomes dry and rough
and tends to catch on fire,
like the grasslands of California
where fire is always a hazard
but it is a different state of mind
to be in a place where you can play
and enjoy the sea breezes
in the fertile valleys
that are so close to the ocean
but still need to be irrigated
so that the ground can support the gardens
that feed an entire nation
and provide the fruits
we enjoy in the winter months.
So much food
they could never eat it all,
so they don't need to hoard it,
they can share it, sell it
and reap great profits in return,
because no one would say
they should just give it all away
because they need to save some
just for themselves,
and they need to get something out of it
just for themselves.
But they seem to be very proud
of all they provide for others,
things from deep inside
the center of that state
and the more taxes that they pay
the more they know they earned that day
but nobody likes withholding money
just to throw it away
with no return on their investment
so sometimes they put it away,
deep in vaults in the biggest banks,
to keep it safe for later,
the way a snail hides in a shell
protected and yet available
ready to come out again
when the rains return
and the soil softens
and the nutrients flow rich and deep.
[*Go to a direct intervention or to trance
termination.*]

11

RESTRUCTURING BODY IMAGES

An inaccurate perception of one's physical appearance and/or an unrealistic image of one's ideal physique often is the basis for self-consciousness, low self-esteem, and behavioral difficulties. The metaphors presented here are used to encourage individuals to bring their perceptions and behavior in line with their physical and physiological realities and also to alter their prejudices about the defects they perceive in themselves.

ALICE IN WONDERLAND

A metaphor about changes in self-perception.

And while you continue to relax,
I can wonder
how Alice in Wonderland felt
as she met all those unusual creatures
and heard all those strange words,
but kept going on her way
not knowing what to expect that day,
not knowing what next or where to do,
might seem to be strange at first,
but after a while
it becomes an adventure
that delights the child
and fascinates the mind,
because you never do know
what's next, what will be,
but you can know
that it is O.K. not to know
what the future holds in store,
because things change over time
and things change in the mind,
as your unconscious mind changes your mind
about how things feel and are,
like Alice when she saw that bottle
that said "Drink Me" on the label,
and when she did
she got larger, then smaller
than she had ever been before,
or at least it seemed that way to her.
And it may be interesting to notice
that when people relax
things begin to change.
One arm may seem higher than the other,
or a leg may seem heavier than before,
and even the entire body
becomes more difficult to find.
It may seem to float at times
or to get smaller and smaller,
as the chair feels bigger and bigger,
or the feet seem to change in some way,
while the hands do it differently,

and after a while you begin to wonder
how you'll ever put it all back together
just the way it belongs.
But how does it belong, really,
and what is the way it should be?
Because tastes change over time,
so what we prefer today
is not what we'll want tomorrow,
and what seems to be exactly right now
may be what is left over later on,
and everywhere you look,
things are changing, rearranging,
so that it is hard to know
what is the way things ought to be.
In summer trees are in full bloom,
though their flowers are no longer there,
and in autumn the green changes,
become reds, oranges, browns and yellow,
and in winter they're all gone,
and begin again next spring,
only now a new limb grows here,
and an old one dies there,
and how should that tree be?
Taller or shorter, more leaves or fewer,
greener or rounder perhaps,
though there are those who might say,
that the tree is just the way it is,
and the way it is
is all it needs to be,
the way they see a newborn child,
each tiny finger exactly perfect,
each tiny ear perfectly exact,
though no two look the same,
like Alice found in Wonderland,
where everything seemed different,
and she discovered how it felt
to love being just what she was.
[*Go to a direct suggestion or to trance
termination.*]

MUSEUMS OF THE MIND

A metaphor about the value of uniqueness.

There is no perfect way to relax
or to enter into trance,
because what happens naturally
is always different each time.
No two snowflakes are exactly alike,
and even the fingerprints of twins differ,
so who's to say which one is the right one,
and which the left?
And so no matter how hard we try,
to do things perfectly,
the odd thing is we always prefer
the thing that is different or unique,
something one-of-a-kind.
Like stamps printed upside down,
or coins made a little bit wrong,
that become prized collector's items,
just because they are different
from all the rest,
even if you need a magnifying lens
to see the imperfection,
because we want to see things differently,
to see things bigger or smaller
than we think they are,
like a mirror in a circus
that changes our shape and form,
so we can really see
what different would be
if different we really were.
Which may explain the collections
in art museums around the world.
On one wall is a Van Gogh,
on another is a Picasso,
and the pointillism of Seurat
stands near the sculptures of Rodin
        sometimes,
their beauty and power stand out,
but everything is out of place
or out of proportion,
two legs different lengths,
two arms, different sizes,

and yet it all is art of the highest form,
the different paintings, different styles,
like clothing styles that change
from one age to another,
and yet each is beautiful and flattering
in its own way.
In the eye of the beholder
every flower is unique,
designed the way it should be
to be exactly what it is,
and that is why we used to play
a game of sorts as children,
to decide which flower we would be
and which we already were,
and then to really look at it later
and be surprised by what we found.
Something you can do as well,
whenever you decide
which flower you belong to,
but for right now
we don't need to know
how you will feel
when you decide to know
that what seems wrong
can be quite right after all,
after you do all your homework
and explore your own museum
in the gardens of the mind
where you can collect
what you need to know
to protect your own treasure
and to treasure what you have collected
even after you think you know
that you do not really know
what they really think
about what you think
about you.
[*Go to a direct suggestion or to trance
termination.*]

THERMOSTATS

A metaphor for self-acceptance.

It is a modern luxury
to be able to have a warm room in winter,
a cool room when its hot outside,
and to be able to set a thermostat
that maintains a constant temperature,
no matter how much the weather changes.
Now we have computer controller devices
that turn off the furnace after we leave,
turn it back on when we come home,
and turn it down again at night,
when we are snuggled under the covers,
all quite automatically.
But all you have to do
is look around the world
to see that things were not always so,
because up north where they have winters
they have learned to use the cold
to create winter carnivals and sports
people down south have never seen.
And even their clothes are different,
warmer and more weatherproof,
because they know they can't change the
    cold
so they use it for all it's worth,
while people in the South
have their own styles
and their own sports,
and in the really hot spots
they barely wear any clothes at all,
and sometimes they don't do anything at all,
because they know that if you can't change
    it,
you'd better not fight it,
and you might as well use it.
So everywhere you go,
even though we can control it inside,
we still can't control it outside,
and if it's not quite right inside,
you can make it warmer or cooler,
but if it's not quite right outside,
then you might as well

make the most of it
and use it to your own advantage
and get used to it
and even like it like that
because that is how it is,
and it always is more pleasant
to want what you've got
and to learn to enjoy it,
unless you decide to move someplace else,
which some people can't do,
and other people wouldn't do if they could,
because they feel at home there,
like they belong there
exactly where they are.
Whether the weather is too hot
or so cold it freezes fire,
they like it like that
and they have found some way
to take full advantage
of just the way it is,
the way movie stars do,
because they come in all shapes
and all sizes too,
with every size nose and ears and eyes,
which they learn to use
to their own advantage,
their own unique quality,
their own special appeal,
that they amplify and enjoy,
and so we do too,
the way we enjoy the snow
or swimming in the surf,
or basking in the blazing sun,
like the locals do,
enjoying what others enjoy,
because they've learned to enjoy
exactly what they have,
so we do too.
[*Go to a direct suggestion or to trance
termination.*]

12

——

UTILIZING
UNCONSCIOUS
RESOURCES

The boundary between the mind and the body is permeable. In other words, the mind can modify or influence virtually any physiological function, from blood flow to the production of antibodies. Although few people know how to accomplish these things consciously, the unconscious mind often can figure out how to do so when given the opportunity.

Anyone genuinely interested in using hypnosis to treat psychophysiological disorders such as ulcers, asthma, arthritis, colitis, migraines, etc. should consult *The Psychobiology of Mind-Body Healing* by Ernest L. Rossi (1986). Rossi's coverage of this topic includes a thorough discussion of the mind-body linkages and a detailed description of his unique hypnotic formula for accessing unconscious solutions. In essence, his approach involves a relatively straightforward request to the unconscious to do whatever it can to resolve the current problem. This request is followed by an expectant pause to allow the unconscious time to determine what needs to be done and to signal its discovery of a solution.

As emphasized in Chapter 2, we recommend that a minimalist approach such as Rossi's be used initially with *all* types of problems. If this minimalist or permissive strategy does not succeed, however, then it may be necessary to employ appropriate metaphorical communications with the unconscious in a further effort to elicit its aid.

CAMP FIRES

A metaphor for ulcers and colitis.

Everyone is familiar
with Smokey the bear,
and his pleas with campers
to make sure their fires are completely out.
So every Scout learns
how to put fires out,
to make sure everything is cool,
nothing left smoldering or hot,
by pouring water on it
or dumping snow on it,
just the way you're supposed to,
keeping it cool
while relaxing in the shade
drinking a tall glass of ice water
and watching that coolness spread,
making sure it is completely out
so you can leave that woods
feeling relaxed and calm
knowing nothing will catch and spread.
Because fire is too hot to handle
unless you're wearing special gloves,
insulated and made of fireproof materials
which used to be very thick and heavy
but now there is a new material
coated with a very thin layer of metal
which is shiny and reflects all the heat,
and keeps everything cool,
even down to absolute zero,
which is as cold as things can get.
But they cool off nuclear reactors
in a very different way,
because when a reactor starts to get hot
it means there are too many electrons
flying around inside,
so they lower in carbon rods
that absorb those electrons,
absorb all that energy,
and as things quiet down
they also cool off,
like turning off a spigot
to quiet that dripping sound,

shutting off the valve
that stops the flow in there.
They can also coat the walls
with something cool and thick,
like they do in houses,
to insulate and protect,
to keep the people inside
comfortable in any weather,
the way skin protects us from many things
but when it gets cut or scratched
it needs to grow back together
to heal that tiny hole,
and so we take care of it,
put a band-aid over it,
and are careful not to bump it,
not to irritate it.
Because it's okay to irrigate things,
to keep them cool and wet,
but we try not to irritate things,
especially not wild animals
that live in forests and parks,
the places we're supposed to protect
by putting those fires out,
the way the rangers do.
Always looking out for smoke
and rushing out to put it out,
before it gets out of control
which you can do too
wherever you go,
wherever you are,
even asleep at night
when those alarms begin to sound,
putting it out without a thought
and returning to a deep, restful sleep,
secure in the awareness,
that you can take care
of *you*.
[*Go to a direct intervention or to trance
termination.*]

PROTECTIVE ANTS

A metaphor for increasing immune system responses to infections.

There is a tree in Africa
that has a special relationship
with a particular kind of ant.
The ants spend their entire lives
living on that tree.
They build their nests
out of its leaves,
they only drink
the particular kind of sap
that tree produces and secretes
or eat the special tiny berries it grows.
They never leave that tree,
because that tree provides
everything they need.
And this type of ant is the only insect
that does live on that tree.
Whenever any other insect
begins to crawl upon it
or lands on one of its leaves
the ant sentries send out an alarm,
and all the other ants come running.
They attack those foreign bodies
and either destroy them
or drive them away
and in this way
they protect that tree
from any invaders
that might attack it
or even destroy it.
They save the tree
and the tree saves them.
There are many other examples
of the same thing throughout the world,
where one tiny creature
protects a large one
from dangerous invaders.
And in each and every case
they always seem to have a way
of paying very close attention
to anything that could be harmful
so that they know immediately
if something is wrong,
and they know immediately
where something is wrong,
and they know what is wrong
and they pay close attention to it
so they can do something about it,
to eliminate it or fix it,
just the way people do
when they notice a pain in a foot
and they pay close attention
to that discomfort
so they can tell what it is
and get rid of that stone in the shoe,
as long as nothing gets in the way,
and they continue to pay close attention
to the way the body reacts
and amplify that reaction
the way they amplify the sound of an engine
to hear what's wrong
and let that body take care of itself
with the same amazing grace
that those ants take care of that tree,
automatically and continuously,
rushing to do those things needed
to heal and protect.
[*Go to a direct approach or to trance
termination.*]

RAFT TRIPS

A metaphor about essential hypertension.

When you take a raft trip,
or drift down a river in a canoe,
you begin to notice things
that otherwise would go overlooked.
Especially those things
that change the flow of the river,
speed it up, or slow it down,
because when the river is wide and deep
the water flows gently along,
and you can lie back,
with your eyes closed,
listening to that quiet sound.
But when the walls of that canyon
begin to close in,
and get narrower and narrower,
the water rushes through faster
and creates dangerous rapids,
that you have to navigate carefully,
until you get back to that place,
where the river bed gets wide again
and deep peaceful quiet returns.
Because water is just like anything else,
the more you compress it,
the faster it goes,
as it flows along,
and the bigger the space it has to fill,
the calmer and quieter it becomes.
And every child knows this, too,
they know when something is too small
that they need to make it bigger
to hold everything they have,
so they get a bigger glass
or they get a bigger bowl
or they get a bigger pair of gloves
so their hands can feel relaxed and
    comfortable,
larger than they felt before,
and everywhere inside
expands to hold it all.

Such a wonderful feeling of relaxation,
like loosening a tight belt
after a huge meal,
and feeling that relief
the pleasure of letting go,
of letting things expand,
feeling the new space provided,
a new freedom to relax,
the kind of quiet calmness you hear
when those noisy children
leave the room and go outside,
and the teacher relaxes,
the pressure relieved.
Even those old riverboats,
with their paddle wheels and steam engines,
could relieve some pressure
by blowing their whistles
when things got too hot inside,
and everyone could relax on deck,
watching the riverbanks go by,
and the slow flow of the water
in the deep channels they followed,
taking their time
to get from here to there,
with nothing to do in the meantime
except relax from the inside out,
and feel the calm stillness
of a quiet pool
moving gently in the moonlight,
while the soft sounds of evening
drift by in an effortless flow,
a calm slowing down
to a gentle softness
as relaxation continues
and becomes a part
of *you*.
[*Go to a direct approach or to trance
termination.*]

WARMING TRENDS

A metaphorical and direct suggestion approach for migraines.

Although pain management is an issue for migraine sufferers, the pain itself seems to stem from intracranial pressure caused by increased blood volume in dilated intracranial blood vessels. By learning how to divert blood flow into the extremities, many individuals become able to alleviate or even prevent their migraines.

Now, while you relax
and allow yourself to experience
the variety of changes that occur
as you drift into a trance,
I would like to help you learn
how to change those things
that will allow you to be able
to prevent or reduce your headaches.
And the thing you need to learn is this,
that when you feel a headache coming on,
what you need to do
is to be able to allow your *hands*, and *feet*,
to become very warm or *hot* very quickly.
So as you pay attention to those hands and
    feet,
I would like you to realize
that you can imagine how it feels
to have those hands and feet
sitting in the hot rays of the sun . . .
or resting in the warm water of a bath . . .
or whatever other image comes to mind
when you begin to pay attention to that
    warmth there,
and begin to feel the warmth grow,
get warmer and warmer, almost hot,
comfortably swollen and warm,
a warmth that may seem to spread
into the arms and legs after a time,
And as that warmth grows
and becomes more clear in your awareness,
you can continue to relax and drift down
into a comfortable trance state
where your unconscious mind can find
its own way to let your mind
become aware of that warmth and heaviness,
a growing warmth and relaxation

in the fingers of that hand
and the other hand,
and the feet in your shoes
and your arms and legs too, perhaps,
heavy and warm, warm and heavy.
That's right,
and from now on
whenever you feel a headache coming on,
what you need to do and can do
is to relax in this way,
remembering the quiet heaviness
and allow that warm thought to return,
greater than before perhaps,
until you feel that warmth everywhere,
or just in those hands and feet,
because now you can buy
gloves and socks
that heat up by themselves,
powered by little batteries
that make those thick gloves warm
and make those soft socks hot,
almost as soon as you put them on,
they begin to get warmer and warmer
you can try them on in a store
and actually feel that heat increase,
as they give off their own heat,
a surprising feeling of warmth
that works so well
they use them in Alaska
where even the bitterest cold
is soon replaced by the pulsating warmth,
as those gloves heat up,
and those socks heat up,
and the hands and feet begin to thaw,
begin to feel soft and swollen and warm,
swollen with a comfortable feeling

that spreads up the arms
and it continues on with you
even after you drift upwards to wakeful
        awareness,
and reach that point where the eyes open.
That's right,
drifting upwards now,
as that warm feeling continues,
a nice warm feeling
that you can create anytime you need to,
anytime you want to.
That's right, a warm wakefulness now,
as the mind drifts up
and the eyes
are allowed to open.

13

IMPROVING
PERFORMANCE

Those who achieve and excel are those who supplement their inherent abilities with an investment of time, energy and faith in themselves. They have a clear vision of their own possible future and they are willing to do whatever it takes to make that vision into a reality. The appeal of that future provides the dedication it takes to practice an activity long enough for the unconscious to master it. Their faith in themselves then allows them to trust their own well-trained unconscious to accomplish their goals. They do not get in their own way and they are rewarded by amazement at their own accomplishments.

Procrastination, lack of motivation and self-consciousness often block performance and prevent people from living up to their own expectations. On the other hand, such phenomena may indicate that their expectations are inappropriate. Before an effort is made to remove such barriers to performance, it should be established that a change to different activities or goals is neither preferable nor possible.

The metaphor scripts presented below are divided into three categories. The first is designed for use with clients who need to do something that they do not really want to do. The second is for individuals who are not motivated to do anything because they do not know what they want. The third is for use with clients who know what they want, have learned how to do it, but would like to improve their performance.

RAISING DOGS

A metaphor about procrastination.

So we won't put it off any longer,
this movement into a deeper trance,
where you can relax completely
and I can explain
to your unconscious mind
a story I heard from a friend
who had a friend whose son was in school
at a distant university.
He was failing his courses
because he would not go to class
and he would not do his homework,
though he said he wanted to,
so he went to see a counselor
who told him to drop out of school
and to raise dogs or lions
because they would growl and attack
if he didn't take care of his business.
This put him off at first,
made him angry,
so angry he just did it,
went to class, did his homework,
got all A's.
And each time he found it hard,
to do what he needed to do,
he thought about raising puppies,
and all he would have to go through
with their little piles here
and their little messes there
as they just did what they wanted to do
whenever and wherever they wanted,
though he did know from experience,
that even a tiny puppy
can eventually be trained
to behave itself, to control itself,
even if it is hard to do
what it really doesn't want to do,
to wait and do it
in the right place at the right time,
because who would want to live with it,
if it never did learn

to behave itself
and to stop acting
like a spoiled soiling pup.
And so even the most rebellious pup
has a willingness to take care of itself
and to just do what needs to be done
if for no other reason than its own comfort,
its own security,
its own sense of self-worth.
And I've often wondered what happened to
      him,
because I know he did not quit school,
and he did not raise dogs,
so I guess he learned his lessons well
and took good care of himself from then on.
[*Go to a direct approach or to trance
termination.*]

HOME

A metaphor for people who are uncertain about their goals in life or in therapy.

And as you relax more and more,
the mind wanders at times,
the way gypsies wander,
from place to place,
never going anywhere special,
just drifting from here to there,
which sounds romantic and relaxing
unless there is someplace, something,
you really want to have,
something you really want to do.
Because it is hard to arrive at your goal
if you do not know where you're going,
if you do not use a map,
but just turn here or there
without planning ahead,
without knowing how to know
what is the right direction for you,
what you really want to do.
Consider the animals of the world,
how they migrate from place to place,
How would it feel to wake up one day
and suddenly feel that feeling
that tells you as sure as sure
that it is time to do something different,
that it is time to fly south,
time to swim north,
time to cross the tundra
or time to cross the ocean,
the feeling that whales feel,
that elk feel, that birds feel,
that king salmon feel and monarch butterflies
        feel,
that horseshoe crabs, and Canadian geese
        feel.
I wonder how it would feel
to know something without knowing why,
to know something with every cell in the
        body,
to know what is wanted and needed,
the way a small child knows,

when it wants a drink of water,
but still does not know what thirsty means.
A craving, perhaps, a desire, a wanting,
the kind of feeling we usually feel
whenever our mind pictures
the kind of meal we crave.
You watch people in a restaurant,
looking over the menu,
trying out different foods in their mind,
imagining the tastes and textures
until they find one that tastes perfect to the
        mind,
like trying on clothes to see if they fit,
or possible futures,
imagining the place and time
that feels, tastes, looks, sounds just right.
That's right, imagining that future feeling
where everything is fine,
and you've finally gotten what was needed,
finally done what was required,
to have that way of being,
to hold that wonderful feeling,
to know there is no need to wonder,
no need to wander any longer,
to know what direction to take
and to enjoy going there from now on,
like a homing pigeon
that somehow seems to know
which way to go to get there,
back where it belongs.
Once it gets its bearings,
knows what direction to go,
it goes there, back there
right to where it needs to be
to be comfortable and happy
and where it belongs.
[*Go to a direct approach or to trance
termination.*]

THE INVISIBLE BARRIER

A metaphor about removing self-imposed obstacles to achievement.

This type of metaphor may be used with all clients in an effort to help them become more willing to achieve their therapeutic goals, or with individuals who have specific goals in mind such as athletes or students.

I wonder if you are familiar with fences,
especially the electric fences used with
    horses.
These fences have a few tiny strands of
    wire,
and through that wire goes a current of
    electricity.
Not the kind of electricity that is dangerous,
just the kind that gives you a jolt,
like static electricity you get from walking
    on rugs,
a sudden, sharp spark.
These wires stretch all around the field,
and as the horses walk from place to place,
they quickly learn where they can go,
and where they don't want to venture.
All it takes is a few brushes against the
    wire,
a few sudden, startling zaps,
and being very smart animals,
they learn to look but not to touch.
They learn so well, in fact,
that after a while,
the farmer can turn off the electricity,
or even replace the wires with string,
and those horses will stay put,
fenced in by nothing at all,
stopped in their tracks by a thought,
by the feeling that some places are off
    limits,
that where they are is safe,
as long as they just stay put,
satisfied to be where they are.
An invisible barrier or boundary
created by the mind,
but once one horse goes through it,
then they all will follow behind,

that barrier shattered and broken,
with no restraints on where they go next.
But where to go next is a problem,
a problem everyone faces,
and not everyone knows how to solve,
which is probably why . . .
you can earn a fortune these days,
telling people their fortunes
and giving advice on what they should do,
We don't know how a horse knows where to
    go,
but we do know
that once they know where they're going,
it is difficult to stop them or rein them in,
because once a tired, hungry horse
sees that stable or barn at the bottom of a
    hill,
all you have to do
is give it free rein
and it will take you there,
as quickly and surely as it can,
because it wants to be comfortable,
and it wants to be fed,
and once it knows where to go
to get what it wants,
even an imaginary boundary
can be leaped over
on the way to that goal.
What fun to hold on tight
and to just let it run
trusting that it will take you there,
swiftly and surely.
That is a pleasure
every child can treasure
if they allowed themselves to do so.
[*Go to a direct approach or to trance
termination.*]

14

DIRECT STATEMENTS
AND SUGGESTIONS

When a client presents one or more of the types of problems discussed in the previous chapters, we typically prefer to begin treatment with the assumption that the client is in a better position than we are to develop a useful solution. This is why we use the Diagnostic Trance first and then a relevant metaphorical anecdote if necessary.

There are times, however, when an optimistic reliance upon the client's unconscious self-healing capacities and the persuasive potentials of metaphorical communications is either unwarranted or inefficient. When metaphors fail to stimulate problem-solving or when the therapist already has in mind a straightforward solution to the problem, then direct statements or suggestions may be the preferred strategy.

Direct *statements* are used to convey a specific understanding, attitude or behavioral assignment. They are not subtle persuasions aimed at the unconscious. They are straightforward messages directed toward both the conscious and the unconscious. Usually, they are messages the client might resist, argue with or ignore in the waking state. However, we have found that these messages are much more likely to penetrate conscious resistances or to "sink in" and have a long-term effect when the client is listening to them from within the relaxed, passive and relatively receptive trance state of mind. Thus, we frequently use the trance state as an opportunity to correct misconceptions, to provide new understandings, to give paradoxical assignments, to assign ordeals, or to make comments designed to elicit rebound effects (i.e., to offer messages that will create the intense emotional reactions needed to motivate the client to take charge of the situation and resolve the problem).

Direct *suggestions*, on the other hand, involve efforts to elicit hypnotically induced alterations in perception, sensation or behavior with the assumption that these alterations will solve or disrupt the problem. Direct suggestions can be very effective when the client is able to comply. Hypnotically induced amnesias can eliminate some sources of discomfort entirely. An altered sense of taste may eliminate smoking or overeating problems. A suggested anesthesia may control chronic pain completely. The list of potential applications is lengthy, but very few novice subjects are able to comply with suggestions for such dramatic hypnotic alterations. For this reason we use them very rarely and include only a few examples in the following scripts.

Direct statements and suggestions may be used in addition to a metaphorical message. We already have presented metaphors for many different types of presenting problems. In this chapter we describe examples of the direct statements and suggestions we might use for some of those problems if necessary. We have observed that a combined presentation of metaphors, direct suggestions and direct statements generally is the most appropriate approach for habit problems and pain management especially. As a result, these two problems are dealt with in separate chapters where scripts are presented which integrate metaphor and direct suggestion.

It should be noted that the scripts for direct suggestions and statements maintain roughly the same rhythm and phrasings that are used for trance inductions and metaphors. The goal is to help the client remain in a trance state while listening to these straightforward messages. Although more emphasis may be added to certain words to enhance the impact of the message, you should be careful not to shift into a conversational pattern which might disrupt the trance and reduce the receptivity of the client.

A DIRECT APPROACH FOR CREATING A PLEASANT EXPERIENCE

Application: May be used at any time with any client. The purpose simply is to give the client a chance to experience something positive in his or her life.

Sometimes later today,
perhaps this evening,
and tomorrow too if you like,
I would like your unconscious mind
to have an opportunity
to give a surprise to you,
a present, a pleasant gift,
something special, something nice,
an unexpected pleasure,
a wonderful feeling,
a particular taste perhaps,
or a brilliant color,
something that suddenly stands out,
and gives you a warm pleasure,
that special feeling
a special treat,
so nice to be alive to experience that,
a brief moment perhaps
or a long one,
a giggle of amusement
or a luxurious sigh.
So keep an eye out for it,
for that time
when your unconscious mind,
sneaks up on you
and opens up your mind
to that special feeling then.
[*Go to trance termination sequence.*]

A GENERIC DIRECT APPROACH

Application: May be used with virtually any client to elicit unconscious assistance in the therapy process.

Tonight, perhaps tomorrow too,
your unconscious can give you a dream,
a very special dream
that clarifies the problem
indicates the source perhaps,
but tells you quite clearly
how to solve that problem now.
And each night afterwards,
until you understand it,
until you decide to do it or not,
that dream can return to you
in one form or another.
And every day
as you go about your business,
your unconscious can find something,
some thought, perception, awareness,
a taste perhaps or a sensation,
or even a color,
that seems familiar
and reminds you of something,
reminds you of what your unconscious mind
is trying to tell you,
until you finally understand
and use that understanding for you.
[*Go to trance termination sequence.*]

A DIRECT APPROACH FOR DEPRESSION

Now, whether you like it or not,
it is entirely up to you,
but if you really want to feel better
what you probably need to do
is to pay closer attention
to what you think
and what you do
because you can choose to think about
        things
that make you sad and feel bad
or you can begin to do things
that make you feel good.
It is entirely up to you.
You can think sad thoughts,
you can remember bad feelings
or you can replace them
with a comfortable participation
in things that you enjoy.
You create the space you live in.
You have the ability
to learn how to direct your thinking
in whatever way *you* choose.
You can change what you do,
you can do things for you.
And so tonight, tomorrow, this week,
what I want you to do is this . . .
Every evening,
when you eat your dinner,
your unconscious mind
can automatically remind you,
perhaps with a particular sound,
a particular thought,
a particular image,
a stop sign of sorts,
an alarm,
that that is the time for you to decide,
what you will do that evening.
You can either decide to do something
        interesting
or something fun for a change,
or you can decide to just sit

and think hard about every unpleasant
        thing,
about everything maddening that has
        happened to you
and about how upset you want to be about
        it.
It's completely up to you,
to enjoy yourself doing something different,
or to practice making yourself feel bad.
[*Go to the trance termination sequence.*]

A DIRECT APPROACH FOR LOW SELF-ESTEEM

It is easy to pay close attention
to things that are wrong.
It's easy to be a critic,
to find fault with everything.
It's easy to not like yourself,
or to not trust yourself to be O.K.
It's harder to have the courage
to see things in a different light.
It's harder to take a risk
and to enjoy yourself,
your life, and other people.
It's easy to find reasons
to not feel good,
to not feel comfortable,
to hide from oneself and others.
It's hard just to say what the heck,
to not care what anyone thinks,
it's hard to give yourself permission
to feel good no matter what,
or is it?
Maybe it's easy,
maybe it's easy to do
but you have been afraid to do it,
because you do know how
and you can do it now
but sometimes it feels wrong
to really believe you're O.K.,
when you might be wrong
but who's to say,
and so from now on,
I want you to know it's O.K.
to do that crazy thing,
to let yourself feel that way.
You can do it now, today,
and you can do it tomorrow.
You can see what is O.K. about you
and what you do.
You can see those things quite clearly,
and feel quite comfortable too.
You can alter your mind
and alter your mood,
even if you have to pretend, for a while,

that this new way of thinking and feeling
is because of something you took
or something that was done to you
and you really can't help it,
that's just the way you feel,
confident, happy and pleased,
until that feeling becomes real.
So do it now,
or just let your unconscious do it for you,
so you don't have to know
what's gotten into you
when your whole way of thinking about you
— *changes!*
[*Go to trance termination sequence.*]

A DIRECT APPROACH FOR ANXIETY

We both know now
that you can scare yourself,
because you have an active mind,
and a reactive body,
and if you think that scary thing
even for a brief moment
it has been scaring you.
But we also both know
that there are other things you can think
that are comfortable and calming,
relaxing and reassuring thoughts or images
that you can use instead
to replace those other thoughts,
to help yourself relax
to maintain that relaxed, calm feeling.
You can let your unconscious mind learn
all it needs to know
to be able to distract you from those scary
        thoughts,
to be able to provide you with those relaxing
        thoughts.
And I think you will enjoy
being happily unconcerned,
unable to remember to worry
in exactly the same way or at the same time.
So from now on,
when you enter that situation,
you can enter it knowing you're protected
and can tell that part of you
that tries to do its job by telling you
that there are things to be afraid of here,
that you really don't need it anymore,
and don't want to hear it anymore,
and so it can either go away
or find a different game to play,
and remind you instead
of the good things that might happen here,
or the fun things that might occur later,
because those old thoughts and fears
aren't useful anymore.
So you can relax and forget it
and go on about your business,

surprised to discover, perhaps,
that you have been thinking
about something else entirely
and you will know at that point,
deep down in every cell of your body,
that you won't ever have to feel that again,
that it is over and done with,
more rapidly than you expected,
not as soon as you would have liked.
You can do it now,
and you can do it later.
You can frighten yourself with that thought,
or you can calmly relax yourself
with a different thought.
That's right,
so practice and choose,
it all belongs to *you*.
[*Go to trance termination sequence.*]

A DIRECT APPROACH FOR MULTIPLE PERSONALITY

Now,
as I speak to each of you together,
there comes a time
when it is time to decide now
how to bring these things together
to join them together as one,
to create a new life,
a new beginning,
not a starting over
but a change of pace,
using what is useful now
and letting go
of the rest of it.
So I would like to say
to one of each of you,
or each one of you,
that I believe you have the ability
to do what I suggest,
to use this opportunity
to evaluate what's there
and to use what is useful
from each one,
to create a new, more complete one,
and to erase the rest,
and to do so very carefully,
with the complete understanding
that each part can be examined,
and some things can be eliminated
while others are blended together
to form a more comfortable you,
to form a more useful you,
to form a happier you
than you've ever been before.
And these things can seem
to happen automatically, almost overnight,
but in reality it happens carefully,
trying on one thing, then another,
until it comes out just right,
then going on with things
better than before,
because things change over time,
come and go over time,
and since things have changed for you

it is time to change you too,
to stay the same from day to day,
to be the same,
to be what you can be
now that you can join,
and say thanks and goodbye to some,
say hello, let's go to others,
and become you, the center of you,
in a most becoming way,
now.
[*Go to trance termination sequence.*]

A DIRECT APPROACH FOR VICTIMS OF ABUSIVE CHILDHOODS

Nothing can undo
what happened to you.
What was done to you
was done *to* you back then.
But that was then and this is now
and you can stop it here and now,
you can stop the pain and fear,
you can put an end to it, *now,*
and you already know how,
you know how to forget to pay attention
to particular things,
you know how to shut doors
and windows on the past,
you know how to see things now
for what they are now, not what was,
and your unconscious knows how to walk
forward in time across that line,
a boundary line
that marks a new beginning,
that lets you join the present,
as you let go of the past,
that lets you see a future, when you will
     remember
how good it felt today
to let go of that past,
to say goodbye to it,
and to let yourself feel O.K.
So go ahead now
and keep going ahead later on,
because that past is through
and you are just you here and now.
And when you get home,
there is something you can do
to put this away and get on with the future,
some way for you, a ritual perhaps,
a ceremonial letting go,
throwing something away
to let yourself know
that the past is done
and the future has begun,
and you will do that,
will you not?
[*Go to trance termination.*]

A DIRECT APPROACH FOR IMPOTENCE AND ANORGASMIA

There is a wisdom to the body,
it knows exactly what to do
to do those things sexually
that you want to have happen,
so I am going to say some things now,
and I want you to pay close attention
to what happens to you,
because you have come here
wanting to be able to respond
and once you learn that you know how
you can never forget how to do it,
you will always know that you know
how to pay attention to that place,
how to realize that you really can feel
everything that goes on there,
every tiny sensation—
every small change in sensation—
that you can watch and see
in the mind's eye now,
as I begin to tell you
that there are certain images you can see,
certain fantasies you can have,
that change those sensations,
make you more aware of things there,
that allow you to put your finger on the idea
that causes you to stir.
Some thoughts enter your mind,
and penetrate deeply into your awareness,
thoughts you ordinarily wouldn't allow
can begin to stimulate imagination,
to arouse your interest in that feeling,
that before you would never notice
in that comfortable, quiet way,
but will later on today, or tonight,
when your unconscious mind
can demonstrate to your surprise
that it knows what to do,
if you allow it to.
It can enjoy creating
those images for you
and let you begin to feel
those thoughts spread down across that line
and grow larger and larger
as it becomes harder and harder
to tell where one begins
and the other ends
as the two begin to touch
in that private, special way,
and at that point you know
that you can leave here today
having learned that you do know
how to feel that special way
very deep within
and again and again,
whenever you want
to allow yourself to do so.
So go ahead now
and discover more on your own,
in your own way,
in whatever way
works for you.
But don't do it too well
or you may have to walk around
excited all the time.
And just imagine what that would be like,
what you might do,
if you were that full of desire.
It could be embarrassing.
[*Pause until client shifts position or shows
some reaction, then proceed to the trance
termination procedure.*]

A DIRECT APPROACH FOR PREMATURE EJACULATION

We tell a small child
to not get so carried away,
to not get so excited
that it ends up yelling and screaming
with happiness and glee.
And I think that every man
should have as much self-control
as a small child.
But it's not like there is something wrong
with being highly sensitive,
or very responsive,
because I am going to suggest
something to your unconscious mind,
that will make it difficult
for you to feel those sensations,
or to respond in that way,
something that will make it hard for you
to have an orgasm at all.
Something you won't hear or understand . . .
consciously,
though your unconscious mind can hear
and can understand and do it now,
and there's nothing you can do,
but I do want you to pay close attention
next time you have sex,
to make sure that the cure
isn't worse than the problem.
Because as your unconscious mind,
makes you feel more and more numb there,
and less and less able
to feel that coming feeling,
you may end up being stuck
with an erection for a long, long time,
too long, perhaps, for comfort.
So I want you to try not to be too worried,
but to worry enough to pay attention
to make sure your unconscious
doesn't do its job too well,
and you end up never coming again,
in which case,
we'll have to try to undo this,
so pay attention and let me know
if you think it's starting
to take too long,
or not happening at all,
even after a lot of effort,
because we wouldn't want you
to forget how to do it . . .
entirely.
[*Go to trance termination sequence.*]

A DIRECT APPROACH FOR UNEXPLAINED INFERTILITY

The next time you make love,
I want you to imagine,
that you are a sexy, turned on teenager,
in the back seat of a car somewhere,
doing things you've never done before,
almost out of control with desire,
letting him do things,
going all the way,
wanting desperately to go all the way,
but hoping and praying first
before you say yes, do it now,
and giving in to it later,
that whatever happens
you don't get knocked up.
I want you
to think about that each time,
just before it's too late to stop it,
that you can't help it,
but do not get pregnant yet
or you will ruin this whole thing,
that would be the wrong thing
to do right now.
Remember that!
Hoping and being afraid
that you might get pregnant
and knowing that would be wrong
right now.
[*Go to trance termination sequence.*]

A DIRECT APPROACH FOR INSOMNIA

So here is what you need to do.
Tonight, and every night this week,
as you lie down to go to sleep,
and pray the Lord your soul to keep,
I want you to try to stay awake
for at least *one long* hour.
And during that time
I want you to think about nothing but blue,
just let your thoughts fill with blue,
and make sure you try to do that for an hour
before you finally let go.
I know it will be difficult,
to experience nothing but the color blue,
but I know you can do it for a while.
So when my words come back to you,
at night as you drift off to sleep,
you will remember to try to stay awake,
at least for a while,
and to be aware only of blue,
like the blue in the sky,
or robin's egg blue
or the deep blue sea.
[*Go to trance termination sequence.*]

A DIRECT APPROACH FOR JEALOUSY

Now you say you are too jealous,
and I know what you need to do
if you really want to avoid that problem
but you won't want to do it
unless you really believe
that she(he) merits your trust,
and so the first thing to do is this:
decide now, here and now, once and for all,
does that person deserve you
and deserve your love, or not? . . .
If they do, then they are trustworthy,
if they don't, then you'd better get out,
right now, as soon as you can,
but if they are trustworthy enough
to deserve you and your devotion
then here is what you need to do,
because your jealousy is the meanest
the most obnoxious thing you can do
to someone who cares about you.
You need to apologize to that person,
in every way you can,
you need to get down on your knees,
and tell him (her) how sorry you are,
for being so mean and cruel,
for even thinking they could betray you,
for not accepting their gift to you,
because if you don't love them,
then let go of them
and if you do love them
then you'd better say you're sorry
and be adult enough
to let them be an adult too,
because if you keep acting
like a mean, suspicious parent
it's quite apparent to me
that you are using your imagination
in a very unpleasant way,
in ways that are quite painful
to those you say you love.
So the first step
is to apologize
for being so mean and cruel,
for using your imagination

in such a childish way,
without any control at all.
And you certainly should apologize
for soiling this sacred ground,
and creating a foul odor
in the atmosphere of love,
because you will feel so embarrassed
if you do it again
that your face will flush,
and you will blush
and that will be the last time
you try to control
what doesn't belong to you
but is a gift, a loan,
that will be repossessed
if you don't treat it right.
So decide now what you're going to do
and what you're not going to do,
and see if you have enough
to do it, no matter what . . . [*Pause*]
[*After several seconds, go to the trance
termination sequence.*]

A DIRECT APPROACH FOR SELF-CONSCIOUSNESS

As you know only too well,
no body is perfect,
but you have yet to be
imperfectly imperfect,
so what you need to do is this
in order to become more comfortable,
this weekend, when nobody will see you,
I want you to buy some bright red lipstick,
the brightest red you can find,
and you rub that lipstick
on that part of you you think is ugliest,
rub it on your most embarrassing part,
and walk around with it red,
red for an entire day,
and every time you see something red,
remember that red place on you.
You will do that,
even though you do not understand why,
will you not?
Good!
[*Go to trance termination.*]

A DIRECT APPROACH FOR PSYCHOPHYSIOLOGICAL DISORDERS

As you relax
in a deep trance now,
deep enough,
I would like you
to give your unconscious mind time
to examine this problem of yours carefully,
until it can find a beneficial solution,
a solution you can use,
a solution it is willing and able to use,
to use for you to solve this problem,
and to solve it comfortably and well,
and when it knows
that it can and will do so,
has decided what to do
and has decided to do it for you,
it can indicate that knowing,
that decision,
by creating a movement
in a hand or a finger,
or an arm may be moved,
or even a leg or a foot,
just some small movement
so that you and I can know,
so that it can indicate
that it knows what to do
and is going to do it.
So let's go ahead
and just wait patiently,
waiting for that unconscious signal,
keep waiting until you know,
until it lets you know somehow,
that it knows how now
and will do it for you . . . [*Pause*]
[*After you detect a small unconscious movement of some sort or a restlessness on the
part of the client, go to the trance termination
sequence.*]

A DIRECT APPROACH FOR PROCRASTINATION

I could tell you
that you will have an irresistible urge
a driving desire to do those things
you complain you keep putting off.
And I could tell you,
while you drift in and out of trance,
that you will get great satisfaction
out of doing those things you haven't,
that nothing else will seem to be as much
      fun,
and that may work,
but the only way we'll know for sure,
is if you do your very best
to fight that idea, that impulse,
and to not do things better for a while,
if you can,
or to not do them very well,
if you must,
because I know it will be difficult
to not do these things for a while,
so I am going to give you permission
to go ahead and do some things,
but just those things you have to do.
So remember to just do what you need
      to do,
and to try to force yourself
to put off everything else,
so that those hypnotic suggestions
have time to build up in force,
while you resist them as much as possible
and just do some things,
whatever things you feel you have to do,
and fight that hypnotic urge
to do everything at once
as much as you can.

A DIRECT APPROACH FOR ESTABLISHING GOALS
(POSTHYPNOTIC PREDETERMINATION)

Application: This approach may be used with clients to determine their preferred life goals or therapy goals and to insert the hypnotic suggestion that their unconscious can take the steps necessary to accomplish these goals. Not recommended for depressed or suicidal clients.

You do not know
exactly what to do
that would allow you
to feel the best you can,
so here is what I want you to do.
I want you to pay close attention
to how you would like to feel,
that feeling of freedom
and calm satisfaction,
the actual physical sensations
that you will feel
when you finally accomplish your goal,
and know you have done so,
have finally gotten things arranged
in the right way for you.
That's right, that all right feeling
as you walk out the door
knowing you've made it,
finally found your place,
and as your unconscious
forms that feeling, that image, that idea,
and sees you there then,
doing and being who you are
when you are what makes you feel best,
it can remember with you
the things you did along the way,
the things you started doing today,
and did a few days from now,
that led you from here to there,
the steps that took you there,
quite automatically and effortlessly.
And as it remembers
what things happened to you,
what things you decided to do,
that let you have that feeling,

that let you accomplish that goal,
I would like it to have the opportunity
to begin to plan how to do that *for* you,
to review the steps needed,
and later on
to take full advantage
of any situation, any opportunity,
to lead you effortlessly,
toward that goal,
a gift, a surprise present
of accomplishing what you need,
without even needing to know
exactly where you're going to go,
just knowing how good you will feel
when you get there . . . [*Pause for 30 seconds.*]
[*Go to trance termination sequence after pausing.*]

A DIRECT APPROACH FOR REHEARSING FUTURE PERFORMANCE

Application: This approach may be used with virtually any therapy client to promote therapeutic progress when the activities needed for that progress already have been identified.

So you know what to do,
you know what needs to be done,
and all you need to do
is to do it right for you,
to let yourself do it
in the way that you can,
so I would like to give you an opportunity
to carefully review and rehearse,
to imagine every movement,
to experience every sound,
to see it all clearly in your mind,
to let your unconscious
go over it with you,
to review and practice it carefully,
step by step,
all the way through,
so that you know
exactly what to do,
and know that you can do it,
and know how you will do it.
So go ahead now,
review every part,
go over it as often as you need to,
to know it is a part of you.
Take your time . . .
do it thoroughly . . .
and when you are through
let me know
by allowing your eyes to open
and wakeful awareness to return.
So go ahead now
while I wait for you
to review it all . . .

15

—

OVERCOMING
HABIT PROBLEMS

People consult a hypnotherapist when they reach the conclusion that they need help solving or eliminating a problem. From their point of view they lack the ability or willpower to deal with the issues themselves. This is especially true when the problem is a long-standing habit problem such as smoking or overeating. Hypnosis often is a last resort in a long chain of efforts to alter such behaviors. Furthermore, many of these clients do not actually want to change their behavior. The habit involved may provide much pleasure, a sense of security, or various secondary gains. These people may be seeking help only because they believe they "should" or because they have been told to do so by a physician, a friend or a family member. They seek out hypnosis because they have the unrealistic expectation that hypnosis itself will somehow magically impose the desired changes upon them.

This belief that hypnosis can force people to change results in several problems. On the one hand, it means that some clients may adopt a totally passive role in the change process. They simply sit back and wait for the hypnotist to impose his/her will upon them. On the other hand, some clients may see the process as a challenge. They virtually dare the hypnotherapist to give them a suggestion they cannot resist or undermine.

The natural consequence of all of this is that most clients with habit problems fully expect the hypnotist to use direct suggestions such as "Chocolate will no longer taste good to you" or "Cigarettes will make you sick." They are on the alert waiting for them and until they hear them they will not relax or feel like they have gotten what they expected or needed. Once passive clients hear a direct suggestion, they tend to relax, comforted by the belief that they now have received a powerful hypnotic suggestion which will take care of the problem for them. Resistant clients, on the other hand, tend to relax once they hear a direct suggestion because they are comforted by the feeling that there is no way the suggestion is going to work.

Unfortunately, direct suggestions are effective in only a small percentage of these cases. Metaphorical suggestions which contain implied directives usually are much more likely to produce long-term change. Direct statements designed to enhance the motivation to change also seem to be more useful than direct hypnotic suggestions. But if the only approaches used are metaphors and direct statements, then these clients are likely to remain in a light trance waiting for the hypnotic suggestions they expect and will emerge from that trance puzzled or disappointed by their omission.

The obvious solution is to blend all of these approaches together, which is why we have not provided separate metaphor, direct suggestions and direct statement scripts for these types of presenting problems. Instead, the scripts contained in this chapter include direct suggestions (which may or may not work, but which do satisfy everyone's expectations), as well as metaphors and direct statements (which are much more likely to foster change). This tandem approach is useful for other types of problems at times, but it seems to be a virtual necessity with habit problems.

The direct statements and metaphors we utilize with habit problems typically are designed to allow the unconscious to confront the client with the negative consequences of the undesirable behavior and/or the positive consequences of change. The unconscious also is indirectly encouraged to create experiences, such as alterations in sensation or perception, which will make it easier to alter the undesirable behavior. Meanwhile, direct suggestions for specific changes in perception or action are embedded within the metaphors. The goal is to appease the conscious expectation of direct suggestions while also setting the stage for other useful unconsciously generated experiences and understandings. This covers all the bases and frequently makes it possible to deal with these problems in one sitting.

A SMOKING ABSTINENCE SCRIPT

Now many people come to me
and ask for help in solving
some particular difficulty,
and they say to me,
"I have no motivation,
I have no discipline!"
And I say to them,
"The unmotivated person
doesn't call for an appointment.
The undisciplined person
doesn't show up on time."
The unmotivated person
does not distinguish the place
they wish to be,
from the place where they are now.
The undisciplined person
stays home.
Now you have all the motivation
you need,
you have all the discipline
you need,
though there is one thing
you still need
which you don't have . . . yet,
and that's self-confidence,
the self-confidence it takes
to set out on a journey
completely prepared for the trip,
knowing you've read the map,
you've charted the course
reservations taken care of,
believing you can, will,
reach your destination
quickly, easily, effortlessly.
The self-confidence it takes
to recognize all the signs of success—
just as now, you recognize
those comfortable hypnotic sensations
in the hands, arms, legs . . .
those physical signs
that allow you to know
you've traveled from one state

to another state
in a calm, confident way.
And you can offer your self
large portions of self-confidence,
large portions of self-esteem,
you can breathe in self-confidence
and breathe out self-doubt
as you continue to enjoy
the journey towards your goal.
Throughout the years
that I have worked with people
I have had many clients come here
with a particularly interesting problem.
They have become obsessed
with the idea of making love
with someone they are attracted to,
and when they've raised the subject
with the object of their desire
they've been told,
in no uncertain terms,
that a physical relationship
was an impossibility.
And the reasons given
for the impossibility have been many:
it is too dangerous or risky,
unhealthy or even unethical.
And yet, faced with all these obstacles,
these clients became more and more obsessed,
convinced that their happiness depended
on the consummation of their desires,
to the neglect of all other aspects
of their lives.
Which reminds me of the man
who had just bought a brand new house,
an expensive house,
in the nicest part of town.
He had admired that house
for many, many years,
maybe since he was a teenager,
maybe from his twenties.
He couldn't remember exactly,
but he did know

he'd been wanting to buy that house
for a long, long time.
And now here it was—all his.
He lavished care and attention on it,
decorated it in tasteful colors
of _____ [*insert colors of client's
    clothing*].
He papered and painted
and hardly paid any attention at all
to that growing headache at first.
In fact, it was several years
before he noticed
that his head seemed to have
a continuous dull ache,
and his muscles were aching as well.
He felt tired a lot, too,
so he visited a doctor
who gave him a prescription,
but he just never felt much better
and everything failed to stop that headache,
or the irritation
and the insidious feeling
that his health was fading away.
But at least he had his house!
And it is easy to understand
how he might feel
if you've ever gone from house to house
real estate open houses perhaps,
or just going to someone else's home,
seeing how the other half lives
can be an educational experience.
But I can understand my client's obsession
with something that's not about to happen,
from the day I saw my dream house.
Of course the price was very beyond
what I could possibly afford,
and yet I couldn't get it
out of my mind.
I imagined myself in the living room,
in the kitchen and in the den
and was certain I must have it
to be happy.
Now everybody knows that no body
likes to be told what to do,

and if I could tell you what to do
you wouldn't have to be here today.
You'd call me on the phone,
you'd say, "I'd like to quit smoking."
And I would say,
"That's a wonderful idea,
quit smoking . . . now."
But every body knows no body likes
to be told what to do,
so I wouldn't say to you,
you already know all the reasons
for ending this smoking problem.
I wouldn't have to say to you that
smoking is dangerous and unhealthy.
I wouldn't have to tell you that you will
receive no pleasure from smoking.
I never need to say that
cigarettes are a poor substitute
for _____ [*insert client's rationale
for smoking, i.e., controlling anxiety,
eating management, boredom, etc.*].
But one thing I *will* say to you is:
"*Not smoking* is not a task
you won't find easy."
And when you leave here today
you'll no longer be
somebody who smokes.
You know you have the desire to smoke,
and you know you know it
and no one can talk you out of it.
But what you now know,
that you didn't know before,
is you also have a large amount
of *no desire*,
and you can get to know this place
of no desire
as it expands and grows
larger and larger.
And the feelings of no desire
can reach deeper and deeper,
the time of no desire continues to lengthen,
and no way is easier than this.
And I read once:
"When I was a child,

I thought like a child,
I acted like a child.
Now that I am grown
I put away the things of childhood."
What does that really mean?
I'm not sure,
but it certainly meant a lot
to my clients who were obsessed with
a sexual desire that could never be fulfilled.
Perhaps it was the thought of putting
old ways behind them
that finally allowed them to be free,
or perhaps they simply grew up
and took responsibility for their feelings
and their behavior.
Disappointment is something we all face
from time to time,
and you can imagine how disappointed
that man was to learn there was insecticide
in the floor and walls of that house.
He went on his dream vacation,
and was amazed to discover his headaches
and sickness disappeared in just
a few days time.
When he got home
he contacted an expert in the field.
The expert gently broke the news,
his entire house was slowly being
        poisoned . . .
and so was he.
It only took him only one day to pack his
        things,
he knew for certain
his health was worth more
than any house—
no matter how long
he'd wanted it.
And I guess I finally came to terms
with the fact that I couldn't buy
a $300,000 home,
no matter what I did.
It was a nice dream,
but the price is too high to pay,
especially since there was no

Jacuzzi!
And it is good
to finally resolve those feelings
and to just let go,
not needing to know
how the unconscious mind knows
what to do . . . for you,
thinking with an awareness
of things thought,
without needing to know
those things which will get done—
automatically,
you know what to do.
Now, I'd prefer
you stop smoking immediately,
but it's entirely up to you
to discover, today,
the best time and way for you.
Some clients wait an hour,
some wait until after dinner,
and some stop entirely right before bed.
Now, I'd prefer you to stop immediately,
but it's completely up to you
to choose the time, a time today,
when you free yourself
from smoking, forever.
[*Go to trance termination sequence.*]

A WEIGHT MANAGEMENT SCRIPT

Now you've been waiting
many years to say
the last word on this subject.
And your last word
is still there . . . in reserve,
spending a life time arming yourself
with final words,
like the forest animals who
store up nuts and berries
for a long winter, or collect
every form of twig, leaf, paper, string
to structure an elaborate nest
as shelter from the winter's cold
or a lurking predator,
real or imagined.
Perhaps a memory of the words
a mother sings to her sleeping child,
rocking, rocking, words
of a soothing lullaby,
full of safety, warmth.
And you can drift away on words,
recalling the word you really want to say
as soon as you get the chance.
And chances are, as you drift
you'll recognize some part of you
that's only just begun
to find a voice,
a voice of confidence and belief
in yourself and your ability
to solve this problem,
once and for all
to exercise your privilege,
your right to have
the body you desire,
and you can offer yourself
large portions of self-confidence,
large portions of self-absorption,
large helpings of self-esteem.
Voicing the part of you
that knows the words
to your body song,
and anyone who gets to know Vivian
knows she spent ten years

of her childhood
taking voice lessons
two or three times a week.
And it was difficult at times
to give up playing with the other kids,
after school to walk
the mile or two a day
to the huge white house
where her singing teacher lived,
until she discovered she could
make a game of it,
wondering as she walked
how persons in so many houses
lived their lives from day to day.
And soon she felt as if
she was not giving up a thing,
not playing with the other kids,
the game she played was so
stimulating and rewarding.
And so when she finally
reached her singing teacher's home
she was completely ready
to begin . . . and to work
on exercising her voice
and learning to manage and use it
exactly as the musical instrument
it was.
Not many people even realize
the multiple and various ways
there are to train a voice,
but she certainly discovered them,
exercising vocal cords
three times . . . fives times a week,
carefully monitoring herself
to nurture herself,
to take care of herself in every way,
and gaining in confidence,
gaining in skill,
gaining in self-knowledge.
As she put every bit of energy
into shaping her voice
into its richest, sweetest tones.
and she sang, publicly

and privately for many years,
and never felt a bit of stage fright,
even when the audience
really couldn't appreciate
the operatic quality of her voice,
and would have preferred
a thinner, less resonant voice.
Of course, for her, it never seemed
a problem
that her voice
was so much bigger than others,
though she knew it sometimes was,
for her high school chorus teacher,
who kept giving Vivian a signal
to tone it down.
She really believed everyone should look
and sound the same,
so Vivian would struggle to fit in,
and sing along, not drawing attention
to herself.
And it wasn't until she went to college
and sang in choruses where everyone
was talented that she knew
it was okay to be more gifted
than the people singing with her.
And she learned that it doesn't matter
if you fit in—in fact
it's much more fun to stand out,
be different, have a particular style
that's all your own.
Now about this business
of losing weight,
you can wait to begin,
but haven't you waited long enough.
When you reach that fork in the road
you know you're going to make a choice
to leave something before you
behind and continue on the journey,
remembering, something you've forgotten
that you know.
Now eating is for pleasure,
and you've forgotten how
to experience the pleasure
of feeling hungry,

the pleasure of feeling full,
the pleasure of feeling satisfied,
the pleasure of saying, "No, Thank You."
No, you eat a lot
but you don't get much pleasure.
You can eat less and get more . . .
pleasure.
You can want less and have more . . .
pleasure.
You can heighten your metabolism,
feel the warmth caressing your skin,
spreading through your arms, your legs,
as you feel the pleasure of
less is more,
as you experience the increased energy
warming you all over,
feeling the pleasure of having
the body you desire,
and you don't have to wait any longer
to exercise your ability, your right,
to gain the body you desire.
Remembering that time
in your life when you knew
how beautiful you are,
recognizing that corpus of knowledge
you have, and
speaking your mind
once and for all,
the reserve of last words
finally voiced,
hearing your voice
as it fills the emptiness with sound.
[Go to trance termination procedure.]

A GENERIC HABIT PROBLEM SCRIPT

Application: For use with any of a variety of habit problems including nail biting, finger sucking, smoking, overeating, etc.

So you've come to see me,
about fixing the problem,
getting rid of this habit
and I would like to tell you
that I am quite impressed
by your willingness to do so,
because it isn't easy
to admit you need help,
it isn't easy
to admit that you have failed
to correct the problem, yet.
But it is clear to me
that you have the ability to do so,
because the people who cannot
do not go to the trouble or expense
of making an appointment,
they just keep telling themselves
that it is silly to seek help
to do something they could do overnight
if they really put their mind to it,
which of course they never remember to do.
But you have come here today
because you really want to get help,
because you really want
to get rid of that habit,
and you've come none too soon,
and it's certainly not too late,
and I know you can change,
I know you can stop that behavior,
because I've seen what people can do.
Why there is even a program
that helps schizophrenics, psychotics,
and people who are brain damaged too,
to learn how to manage their behavior,
which is very difficult for them.
A simple program designed by a Dr. Zec,
it consists of nothing more
than writing down what they want to
    change,

then writing down the steps involved,
the specific things they need to do
to accomplish their goal.
And then they write down why,
they write down why they should,
the benefits of that change,
as many as they can think of.
They write them down
and then each day
they look at that thing they want to do,
they look at the specific steps involved
and they look at why they want to do it,
to remind themselves.
And all this writing down
is necessary for them, absolutely necessary,
because they can't remember
from one day to the next
what it is they meant to do
or why they wanted to do it,
or what they needed to do
to accomplish that goal,
they can't remember it,
because they are handicapped in some way,
which makes it a pleasure
to work with you,
because I know that you
will remember what you want to do
and *why* to do it, and *how* to do it,
so I don't have to make you
write it all down in detail
or look at it every day,
except in your mind, your unconscious mind
    perhaps.
I can just ask you to think it through,
to define what you want to do, exactly,
to look at how to do it exactly,
what you need to do each moment of every
    day
and I know that you

will remember it thoroughly later on.
And I also know
that if Dr. Erickson were here today,
he would tell me
that I really don't need to tell you
that you won't do that anymore,
that you'll find it easier to not do it,
because now you know
what you're not going to do
and you know how to not do it
all by yourself, reminding yourself,
but he might say to you
in a way that would reach into your
        unconscious
and create an irresistible response
that no matter how hard you try
you'll never be able
to _____ [*insert undesirable habit*]
        again,
in exactly the same way, or at all,
without noticing how unpleasant
it seems to make you feel,
which you had probably overlooked before,
or forgot all about,
but not as much forgetting
as the people I mentioned before,
who have a disability in that arena,
which is why they write it down
which reminds me of a man I saw on TV
who forgot to live his life.
He went to work every day,
he stayed home every night,
he saved money for his retirement,
when he would finally do what he wanted.
But when he retired
he found out he had cancer,
only a few months left to live,
and he cried as he talked
and said he'd wasted his entire life
putting off what he wanted to do,
ruined it by forgetting
to pay attention to what he did each day,
and to give himself strict orders
to take care of himself now,

to be good to himself now,
which is not the same
as being forced to eat your spinach
or told never to give yourself a treat,
but some people have to write it down
before they get the point
that now is the time to do
what you can do or can not do
that you have decided to do for you.
So you can leave here today
with the full recognition
that you can remember what to do,
and that not remembering
is not something you'll find easy,
because now it belongs to you,
even after you leave here
it will be there with you,
the memory of an ability
to find a different way
to do those things for you
that *it* used to do
but can't do now, anymore,
because now if you do it
you'll be doing it on purpose,
and that's not the same, is it?
So I would rather you stop now,
and remember to keep on stopping,
but you may prefer to stop
tonight at bedtime,
or an hour from now,
just so you can remind yourself
what it is you can remember
that those other poor people
had to write down
before they did it,
successfully,
so of course
so can you,
will you not?
[*Go to trance termination process.*]

16

MANAGING PAIN

The scripts presented in this chapter are examples of an entire hypnotherapy session for pain management, including the induction, metaphorical implications, direct suggestions and trance termination procedures. These scripts reflect the fact that hypnotic intervention for physical pain usually is a much more straightforward procedure than hypnotherapy for emotional or psychological suffering.

Pain and pain management are complex topics which extend far beyond the scope of the material presented here. Before you attempt to use hypnosis for pain management training, you should become familiar with the available literature. In the meantime, however, there are several points worth stressing.

First of all, pain is only a signal, a neurophysiological event which must be noticed and interpreted cognitively before it turns into suffering. Suffering stems from the anger, fear and other reactions people experience when they cognitively interpret pain. Morphine, for example, does not "kill" pain. Rather, it puts people in a state of mind where they no longer care about it or think about it. The pain signal is still there but it no longer concerns them. Thus, when you eliminate the negative cognitive connotations of the pain, much of the emotionally based suffering is eliminated as well.

Hypnotic trance can be used to reduce negative connotations and suffering. In a relaxed trance people can learn to remain calm and unaffected by a sensation that otherwise might terrify or enrage them. They also can learn to redefine their pain as an itch, a cramp or a hot sensation. Sometimes they even can learn how to not experience it at all. They can disconnect from it or simply "forget" how to locate it.

Secondly, pain can be a meaningful signal or it can have no value at all. If the sensation is an alarm which means that something is wrong physically which can and should receive attention or if it means that tissue is being destroyed, then it is meaningful.

It is difficult and potentially dangerous to ignore or eliminate a meaningful pain signal. By definition, meaningful pain is an alarm calling attention to a situation which requires corrective action. On the other hand, a pain in an amputated foot or the pain originating from a strangulated nerve which cannot be corrected is meaningless. The short-term pain from a surgical procedure, a dental procedure, or childbirth also usually lacks real significance. Although there is damage being done, there is no reason to attend to it. Awareness of the pain will not improve an operation and lack of awareness will not ruin it.

As long as a patient believes that a pain is important or meaningful, it will be difficult for that person to learn how to use hypnosis to manage the experience of it. For example, one patient was able to learn how to reduce his discomfort only after he was thoroughly convinced that the sharp twinges he felt did not mean that bone fragments slowly were severing a nerve in his injured back. Patients need to be consciously reassured prior to the use of hypnosis that an inability to feel a sensation will not result in any undue damage. So do hypnotherapists.

When a pain does have meaning, care must be taken to preserve the cautions or restrictions created by that signal even as you reduce the suffering. Various types of back pain, for example, serve as a warning not to move in certain ways or not to lift too much weight. Ignoring these signals could result in serious muscle, nerve or disc damage. Instead of attempting to block these signals out entirely, an effort can be made to transform them into alternative protective signals such as tightness or warmth.

Finally, pain may be a short-term, situation-specific phenomenon or it may be a long-term, chronic experience. A short-term discomfort can be managed rather easily by most people. Chronic pain, however, carries with it the memory of past pain and the anticipation of all future pain. The hypnotic approaches used to deal with these two different types of pain must take into account these differences as well as the meaningfulness of the pain signal itself. Thus, we provide different scripts for chronic versus acute pain.

Because chronic pain patients automatically will be drawn into an awareness of their pain as soon as they are told to close their eyes or relax, the pain itself is used as their initial internal focus. By directing attention toward the pain while at the same time encouraging relaxation and calmness, one can allow patients to learn that the pain signal will not destroy them. This removes the tendency to struggle angrily or fearfully against the pain, which can itself cause muscle cramping or spasms and further pain. As patients learn that they can be highly aware of the pain and yet remain calm, their suffering diminishes. Treatment then becomes a matter of guiding them through a series of internal events (images, thoughts, perspectives, etc.) until one or more is found which creates the comfortable relief sought. An opportunity to practice using these newly discovered abilities is provided before they are brought out of trance. It should be apparent that there is a tremendous similarity between the steps in this process and the steps in hypnotherapy. The logic, goals and procedures of each are virtually identical.

The procedures typically used to help patients prepare to control an anticipated short-term pain also involve a brief trance induction followed by a series of comments or suggestions designed to enable the person to recognize different ways that sensations can be altered or numbness created. The effectiveness of these approaches cannot be directly monitored by the subject because pain is not present. Hence, the therapist may provide a painful stimulus or direct the client to do so in order to "test" the degree of pain control created. The discovery of an effective approach is followed by a practice session wherein the pain control is successively removed and reinstated until the subject has mastered the internal "shift" which produces the desired lack of sensitivity. This procedure is comparable to the rehearsal procedure used during the trance termination phase of hypnotherapy.

CHRONIC PAIN MANAGEMENT SCRIPT

Applications: For use with long-term pain such as back injuries, nerve damage, phantom limb pain, cancer, etc.

With your eyes closed,
as you begin to relax,
you probably notice
that the first thing you notice
is how difficult it is
to not become aware
of that pain and discomfort,
and that's fine.
You don't need
to fight your mind
which is always aware
of those sensations there
for you
because as you relax,
you can begin to discover
that each time you relax
a muscle in an arm . . .
or a leg . . .
or your face . . .
or even a foot . . . or a finger,
that you can drift down
more and more deeply than before,
into that sensation there
in a more relaxed and comfortable way.
Because there really is no need
to make the effort it takes
to try to stay away
from that feeling
or to try to fight that feeling,
which almost seems to guide and direct
awareness down toward it,
more and more into it,
and as you drift toward it,
toward that center of that feeling,
everything else
can be allowed to relax,
to relax more and more,
as you begin to discover
that it really is O.K.
to let go in that way,

to allow yourself to relax
every other part of your body
and to drift down toward
the very tiniest center
of that feeling
the very small middle of it,
the source of it,
and then to drift down through that center
into a place beneath it
of quietness and calm awareness,
down through that feeling,
and out the other side,
into a space of relaxed letting go,
of comfortable relaxation,
where the mind can drift,
the way waves drift
from one place to another
as that body relaxes
and the mind becomes smoother and
     smoother,
able to absorb events, even those events,
easily and comfortably.
To become absorbed
in thoughts and images,
as the mind reflects
the clear wonder of a child,
a young child,
watching a flock of geese
as they soar
across the sky
and fly into the mists,
the rhythm of their sound
becoming softer and softer,
as soft as the down
in a pillow in a place
where you rest and relax,
a most comfortable place
for a child to relax
and drift in dreams
through the mind, protected and safe.

Where letting go
allows the flow and the soft floating upwards,
where the mind drifts free
of things far below,
and seems to soar
in a sky as clear as glass,
so smooth and clear
that it disappears
when you look at it,
and what appears instead
is the deep blue shine
of the warm soft sun,
a star far beyond
that reaches out and provides
that warm soft light
as you drift down
and experience the comfort
and learn to feel the sound sleep
that your unconscious mind
can provide to you
whenever you relax
and allow it to drift into a trance.
Because it can take you
down through that feeling,
into a space,
that relaxed comfortable place,
as you relax
and allow it to do so
just for you.
That relief and relaxation,
that drifting down through
which comes to you
whenever you allow it to,
just as that drifting upwards
occurs as well,
a drifting back
toward the surface of wakeful awareness,
as your unconscious mind
reminds you to drift up
in a relaxed, comfortable way.
Back toward the surface now,
bringing with you
that comfortable relaxation,
that automatic change in sensation,
even as the mind drifts upwards,

the relaxation continues,
as the mind awakens
and the eyes open
but the body remains behind, relaxed.
That's right, eyes open now [*pause*]
but before you come back completely,
you can close those eyes again,
and feel that relaxation again,
and recognize that ability,
that ability to relax,
to let your unconscious mind
find the way to provide you
with more and more comfort,
more and more relaxed, letting go.
That's right.
Aware that you can do so,
anytime, anyplace you need to or want to,
you can return to that place.
So here is what you do,
later on today, tomorrow, next week
and for the rest of your life,
whenever you need to or want to,
you can close your eyes
just for a moment, perhaps,
and feel that comfortable feeling,
that change in sensation,
returns to you
and you drift into that light trance
or a deep trance
where your unconscious mind
can take care of you,
make things comfortable for you,
and then you return
to the surface of wakeful awareness,
not needing to make the effort it takes
to try to tell if that feeling is there or not,
just as you return now
back to the surface,
comfortably rested and refreshed,
remaining relaxed perhaps,
even as the eyes open again,
and wakeful awareness returns,
now!!

ANTICIPATED SHORT-TERM PAIN MANAGEMENT SCRIPT

Applications: For use with childbirth, dental work, surgery, sports injuries, etc.

Now, your eyes are closed,
and you are sitting there comfortably aware
that you have come here today
because you want to learn
to use your own hypnotic abilities,
to eliminate some future sensation of
     discomfort.
And so, as you begin to relax
and to drift down into a light trance,
or a medium trance,
or even a deep trance,
I want you to take your time doing so.
Not too quickly yet,
because there are some things
you need to listen to carefully first.
For example, you need to understand
that you already have an ability
to lose an arm or a hand,
to become completely unaware
of exactly where that arm is positioned,
or the fingers,
and you have an ability to be unconcerned
about exactly where that finger went
or that hand or leg,
or your entire body,
which may seem to take
too much effort to pay attention to at times.
Because you also have an ability,
an unconscious ability
you can learn how to use,
and that ability is the ability
to turn off the feeling
in an arm, a leg, or anywhere.
And once you discover how it feels
to not feel anything at all,
wherever you want that to occur
then you can create the numb, comfortable
     feeling
anywhere, anytime it is useful to you.
And I don't know whether your unconscious
     mind

will allow you to discover that numb feeling
in the right hand, or a finger of the left hand
     first,
a tiny area of numbness,
a comfortable tingling feeling,
a heavy, thick numbness,
that seems to grow and spread over time,
until it covers that hand, the back of the
     hand,
or anything else you pay close attention to,
it just seems to disappear from your
     experience.
But you don't know how it feels,
to not feel something that isn't there,
so here is what I want you to do.
I want you to reach over to that numb area,
to that numb hand,
that's right, go ahead and touch it,
and feel that touching
as you begin to pinch yourself there,
a sensation you may feel at first,
but as you continue to pinch yourself,
an interesting thing happens . . .
you begin to discover that there are times,
when you feel nothing at all there,
that's right, sensation just seems to disappear,
as you learn how to allow
your unconscious mind
to turn off those sensations for you.
All you need to do is just pay attention,
pay attention to that numbness.
And as that ability grows and develops,
and you begin to know, *really* know,
that you already do know
how to allow sensation and pain to disappear
from that hand there, or anywhere,
your other hand can return to its resting
     position. . . .
and you can drift up to that point
where wakeful awareness will return.
So go ahead now, as you relax,

and discover how to let go
and to feel that numbness more and more
    clearly,
and then you can drift up,
in your own time,
in your own way.
That's right, take your time to learn,
and then drifting back upwards, eyes opening.
[*Pause and allow the self-practice to
continue until the client opens his/her
eyes. Then immediately continue.*]
Now, before you wake up completely,
I would like you to close your eyes again,
and allow that drifting down again,
reentering that place of calm relaxation,
because there was a young boy on TV
not long ago,
who had learned how to control *all* of his
    pain.
he described the steps he went down in his
    mind,
one at a time down those steps,
until he found this hall at the bottom,
like a long tunnel,
and all along the tunnel on both sides
were many different switches, switchboxes,
each clearly labeled.
One for the right hand, one the left, one the
    leg
and one for every other place on the body,
and he could see the wires to those switches,
the nerves that carried sensations
from one place to another
all going through those switches.
And all he needed to do
was to reach up in his mind
and turn off the switches he wanted to
and then he could feel nothing at all
no sensation could get through from there,
no sensation at all,
because he had turned off those switches
    there.
He used his mind's abilities differently
from the man who simply made his body
    numb.

He didn't know how he did it exactly,
all he knew was he relaxed and disconnected,
like a train car disconnecting from the rest,
moved his mind away from his body,
moved it outside someplace else,
where he could watch and listen,
but drift off someplace else.
And it really doesn't matter
exactly how you tell your unconscious what
    to do,
or how your unconscious does it for you.
The only thing of importance
is that you know you can lose sensations
as easily as closing your eyes,
and drifting down within
where something unknown happens
that allows you to disconnect,
that allows that numbness to occur,
and then a drifting upwards now,
upwards toward the surface
and slowly allowing the eyes to open
as wakeful awareness returns
with a comfortable continuation
of that protected feeling
of safe, secure relaxation
and an ability to forget an arm,
or anything at all,
with no need to pay attention
to things that are just fine,
that somebody else can take care of
while you drift in your mind
and then return when it is time
to enjoy that comfortable drifting upwards
where the eyes open
and wakeful awareness returns
quite completely *now*.

17

—

TRANCE TERMINATION PROCEDURES

It is possible to end a hypnotherapy session by saying simply, "Okay, it is time to quit now, so go ahead and wake up completely and open your eyes." However, such an abrupt ending provides no time for rehearsal of new learnings, ratification of the trance experience, or distraction of the conscious mind. It also may leave the client feeling a bit disoriented or dazed.

The comments presented below are designed to lead the subject gradually back to wakeful alertness, to provide an opportunity for reviewing and integrating new learnings, and to create an experience which validates the trance as an atypical state of mind. Instructions also are given for procedures designed to distract conscious attention and "seal off" the trance as a separate phenomenon before follow-up questions are asked. It is best to follow each of these steps in the trance termination process when ending a hypnotherapy session, even if that session involved only a light trance.

STEP I: REVIEWING AND REHEARSING TRANCE LEARNINGS

And so,
before you allow yourself
to drift up completely
into conscious, wakeful alertness,
it may be useful for you
to utilize the opportunity now,
to think about what you've experienced,
the thoughts, images, understandings,
and how you might use these things later on
from one day to the next.
Because you have an unconscious mind
and you have a conscious mind,
and those two minds can learn,
from your experiences here today,
some things that you can utilize
to deal more effectively with those things
that have been problems for you before.
And so before you continue to drift up
into conscious awareness,
normal wakeful awareness,
it is your privilege
to use this comfortable self-awareness
to become more aware of those things
you can use later on,
those learnings,
abilities and skills
you may have overlooked before,
to give you a new view
of the possibilities for a new way
of thinking and feeling and doing things.
That's right, take some time now,
a brief time that seems to be a long time,
to review and plan,
at some level of awareness,
those things you will do later on,
those things you may change later on,
as you begin to use more and more of *you*.
[*Pause for several seconds, then continue*
with the ratification suggestion.]

STEP II: RATIFICATION SUGGESTIONS

You can use that time now,
because in a few moments from now,
when you drift up and awaken,
it may be interesting for you to know
that in that drifting, relaxed state of mind,
where thoughts drift by like dreams,
that enter awareness for a time
and drift through the mind,
while some are left behind,
to be utilized later on,
and others are remembered,
or seem to be remembered at first
but then become more and more distant,
    forgotten over time,
and the entire experience
can seem so far away,
as your unconscious mind
protects the conscious mind
and leaves those things, behind,
forgotten but remembered too.
And time changes too,
so you can know
what a trance it's been
when you begin to know
that what seemed to take a short time,
turns out to have been a long time,
or what seemed a long time,
was really no time at all.

STEP III: REORIENTATION TO WAKEFUL AWARENESS

So for now,
as the unconscious mind
allows the conscious mind
to become more aware of sounds,
sounds in the room, the sound of my voice,
[*Voice volume and tempo*
of speech should be increased
a bit at this point.]
the sensations in an arm, a leg,
the variety of thoughts and feelings
as the conscious mind drifts up

[*Pause briefly to allow the client to finish*
opening his/her eyes. Many people begin
moving and stretching at this point whereas
others simply open their eyes and remain
motionless. In either case, move on to the
distracting comments shortly after they have
opened their eyes. All post-trance comments,
including distractions, should be offered in a
normal conversational tone of voice.]

and conscious wakeful awareness
returns quite completely *now*.
Up to the surface of wakeful awareness,
restfully refreshed, comfortably awake,
even as the mind drifts up completely
and the eyes . . .
are allowed to open *now* . . .
That's right, eyes open,
and wakeful awareness returns
quite completely *now*. . . .

STEP IV: DISTRACTIONS

There are innumerable possible distracting comments. What follows is a brief description of several types. Use your own creativity to generate a new one for each session.

A. *Back to the beginning*—This type of distracting comment continues a previous conversation or refers back to an incident which occurred prior to the trance induction process. As the client focuses upon the threads of this pre-trance memory, he/she tends to lose track of the memories about the intervening trance process.

Examples:

—"Now you say that _____ [*insert any topic the client mentioned prior to the induction*].
—"But I do think it might be important for you to examine your feelings about _____ [*again, insert a previously discussed topic*].
—"It also occurs to me that _____ [*insert a follow-up observation regarding a previous topic*]."

B. *Non sequiturs*—These comments are so irrelevant to the current situation that they take the client by surprise. The resulting confusion prevents undue cognitive processing of the preceding trance experience.

Examples:

—"I really like your [*shoes, shirt, tie, dress or any article of clothing the client is wearing*]! Where did you buy it?"
—"What do you think about that [*lamp, rug, chair or any object in the office*]? I've been thinking about replacing it."
—"Do you know what the weather forecast is for tomorrow?"

C. *Future Plans*—These comments encourage the client to review his/her plans for the future and thus discourage reviews of the immediate past. Again, a partial amnesia for the trance is the usual result.

Examples:

—"So, what are you planning to do this weekend?"
—"Good, let's discuss a time for our next appointment. How would it be if we met on _____ [*specify a day and time*]?"

D.   *Ratifications*—Some comments or questions not only serve to distract the client from reviewing trance events, but also tend to ratify the trance at the same time.

Examples:

—"Hello! Welcome back. How was your trip?"
—"Do you really think you are completely awake yet or should I give you a few more seconds to pull yourself back together more completely?"
—"Are your hands and legs still feeling a bit strange?"
—"Now, how long do you think you were in that trance? How long has it been since we started?"

STEP V: FOLLOW-UP QUESTIONS

Once the client has been distracted from an immediate analysis of the trance, it is safe to probe for feedback regarding the experience. Insights and decisions which should remain in the protective realm of the unconscious for the time being will have receded. The remaining conscious memories can be used to determine which internal events captured the attention of the conscious mind most dramatically and what external events seemed to disrupt the process. This information, in turn, can be used to improve the effectiveness of future hypnotherapy sessions.

Examples:

—"Is there anything in particular that you would like to mention about that experience?"
—"What do you remember most clearly about that experience?"
—"I would like to find out a bit about what happened to you, such as what was most interesting or pleasant to you and what, if anything, seemed to disrupt the process."

Some clients find it difficult to put their experiences into words at first and others seem reluctant to discuss the process at all. These post-trance responses should be respected and no effort made to probe for additional information. Similarly, clients who wish to discuss the hypnotherapy experience at length should be allowed to do so.

As mentioned in Chapter 2, it must be realized that assessments of the therapeutic impact of a hypnotherapy session cannot be based upon these post-trance reports. Clients may report that nothing of significance happened to them while at the same time they are saying things which clearly reflect a significant change in attitude or perspective. Furthermore, the effects of a hypnotherapeutic intervention may not become apparent until several days or weeks after the session. The purpose of post-trance questioning is merely to determine what facilitated or inhibited the trance experience for the client, not to determine therapeutic effect. Therapeutic effects will be reflected by subsequent changes in affect, cognition or behavior, not necessarily by the client's post-trance reports.

After you have completed the steps involved in trance termination you may conduct the remainder of the session in whatever way you choose. The hypnotherapeutic approach described in these pages is an adjunct to your other psychotherapy techniques, not a replacement for them. Use hypnotherapy when it seems appropriate to do so, but do not be misled into thinking you can rely exclusively upon it. In order to be effective, it must be used within the context of a positive psychotherapeutic relationship.

POSTSCRIPT

New clients often ask if we ever get tired of listening to the same problems day after day. Evidently it is difficult for them to believe that therapy can be a constant source of fascination and satisfaction. But within the framework of the approach described here, each new client offers a new and completely unique opportunity to reexperience the wondrous complexity, the perfect harmony, and the vast potentials of every human being on this planet.

When we conduct a Diagnostic Trance, our clients give us the privilege of entering into that previously unseen inner world with them. They take us where their pain takes them and we are allowed to share their amazement as understanding replaces confusion. Some clients prefer to keep that inner world private, a secret even from themselves, perhaps, and with these clients we are taught a reverence for the Self and an acknowledgement that not all knowledge needs to be conscious knowledge.

Above all, however, our clients consistently demonstrate to us the self-healing, growth-seeking potentials within us all. Hypnotherapy merely sets the stage and provides an opportunity for change. Like masters of improvisation, clients seize the opportunity and utilize it in their own creative ways to relieve their pain and to foster change. Each client is different, each situation is different, and what each client needs in each situation is different. The marvel is that almost all of them can find and use what they need when given the right opportunity and encouragement to do so.

When you incorporate hypnotherapy into your practice, you will enter into a new relationship with your clients. Like an orchestra conductor or a master playwright, the hypnotherapist creates an atmosphere which often evokes transcendent thoughts, intense emotions, and powerful insights. Primarily, however, hypnotherapy involves a mutual recognition and celebration of the client's inherent potentials and abilities. By agreeing to rely upon these unconscious capacities for understanding and relief, both you and your client agree to trust that client's resources completely. As a result, the respect and admiration you demonstrate for each client by using these hypnotherapeutic procedures establish a strong precedent for that individual's personal sense of competence and self-reliance.

This brings us to our concluding observation. Although we have endeavored to provide hypnotherapy scripts that we have found to be useful with many different types of clients, it must be emphasized again that these scripts were designed to serve as templates or examples. To the extent that they are relevant to the needs and dynamics of any given individual, they may prove to be therapeutically useful. On the other hand, we encourage you to begin as soon as possible devising metaphors and phrasings for each of your clients which are specifically selected to express the unique problems and personality of that client and your own unique style as well.

Our initial injunction to workshop participants to trust their unconscious probably did not work very well because their unconscious minds had not yet had an opportunity to learn what was needed. Practice using the materials presented here until you have developed a familiarity with the concepts and processes, then trust your unconscious. Its powers of observation, comprehension and creativity may surprise you and your clients as well.

APPENDIX A

*Results of the Research
Project to Study the
Effectiveness of Scripts*

The subjects for this study were 13 graduate students in psychology and related fields who volunteered to participate in a free one-day workshop and research project on hypnotherapy. Following a didactic training session, the participants were randomly divided into a script condition (n=7) and a no-script condition (n=6) and were instructed to pair up and take turns inducing hypnotic trance with arm levitation. The subjects in the script group simply read the script. The subjects in the no-script condition made it up as they went.

Each of the 13 participants completed a five-item questionnaire prior to the workshop and immediately following his/her practice session. The questionnaire asked the participants to use a four-point scale (1 = poor, 4 = excellent) to rate: 1) their skills in hypnotic induction, 2) their ability to elicit an arm levitation, 3) their self-confidence in their ability to induce a trance, 4) their comfort with using hypnosis in an actual clinical setting, and 5) the odds that they actually would attempt to use hypnosis in a clinical setting. In addition, after a participant had served as a practice subject, he/she was asked to complete a questionnaire regarding the depth of trance experienced (1 = none, 4 = very deep), the degree of lightness or lifting experienced in the arm (1 = none, 4 = very strong) and any increase in understanding of trance as a result of that trance experience (1 = none, 4 = very great).

The results are presented in Tables 1 and 2. Briefly stated, the pre-workshop self-ratings of the participants eventually assigned to the script condition did not differ

Table 1
Self-Ratings as a Hypnotist

Variable Rated		Script N = 7 $\overline{X}$	S.D.	No Script N = 6 $\overline{X}$	S.D.
I. Skills in hypnotic induction	Pre	1,714	.488	1.667	.816 (N.S.)
	Post	2.857 (p<.01)	.377	2.333 (N.S.)	.516 (p<.05)
II. Ability to elicit an arm levitation	Pre	1.429	.534	1.167	.408 (N.S.)
	Post	3.143 (p<.01)	.690	1.833 (N.S.)	1.329 (p<.05)
III. Self-confidence in ability to induce trance	Pre	1.714	.756	1.667	.816 (N.S.)
	Post	3.143 (p<.01)	.690	2.166 (N.S)	.752 (p<.05)
IV. Comfort with ability to use hypnosis in a clinical setting	Pre	1.714	.488	1.500	.548 (N.S.)
	Post	3.000 (p<.01)	.577	2.000 (N.S.)	.894 (p<.05)
V. Odds of attempting to use hypnosis in a clinical setting	Pre	1.714	.756	2.167	.983 (N.S)
	Post	3.429 (p<.01)	.787	2.500 (N.S.)	.837 (p<.05)

Table 2
Self-Ratings of Hypnosis Subjects

Variable Rated	Script N = 7 $\overline{X}$	S.D.	No Script N = 6 $\overline{X}$	S.D.
I. Depth of trance	3.000	.577	2.333	.516 (p<.05)
II. Degree of arm levitation experienced	3.714	.488	2.000	1.095 (p<.05)
III. Learning from the trance experience	3.429	.534	2.667	.516 (p<.05)

significantly from the pre-workshop self-ratings of the participants eventually assigned to the no-script practice condition. By the end of the workshop, however, the self-ratings of the participants who used a script had increased significantly on each item (p's < .01) whereas the ratings of the participants in the no-script practice condition had not changed significantly. Along the same lines, the post-practice ratings obtained in the script condition are significantly higher than the post-practice ratings of the no-script participants (p's < .05).

These increases in self-confidence may be attributable to the simple fact that the script worked and the unstructured practice did not. This is reflected by the ratings obtained from the hypnotic subjects during these practice conditions. Ratings of trance depth, arm levitation and learning from the experience all were significantly higher in the script condition than in the no-script condition (p's < .01).

The results of this simple study confirmed our hypotheses regarding the potential value of hypnosis scripts as a means of increasing skills and self-confidence. They also supported our decision to provide scripts for every step in the hypnotherapeutic process. This book is the product of that decision.

REFERENCES

Erickson, M. H. (1980). *The Collected Papers of Milton H. Erickson on Hypnosis. Vol. III: Hypnotic Investigation of Psychodynamic Processes.* (Edited by Ernest L. Rossi). New York: Irvington Publishers.

Erickson, M. H., Rossi, E. L., & Rossi, S. I. (1976). *Hypnotic Realities: The Induction of Clinical Hypnosis and Forms of Indirect Suggestion.* New York: Irvington Publishers.

Fisch, R., Weakland, J. H., & Segal, L. (1982). *The Tactics of Change.* San Francisco: Jossey-Bass Publishers.

Fodor, J. A. (1983). *The Modularity of the Mind.* Cambridge, MA: The MIT Press.

Gazzaniga, M. S. (1983). Right hemisphere language following brain bisection: A 20-year perspective. *American Psychologist, 38,* 5, 525-537.

Gazzaniga, M. S., Bogen, J. E., & Sperry, R. W. (1967). Dyspraxia following division of the cerebral commissures. *Archives of Neurology, 16,* 606-612.

Haley, J. (1985). *Conversations With Milton H. Erickson, M.D. Vol. 1: Changing Individuals.* New York: Triangle Press.

Havens, R. A. (1985). *The Wisdom of Milton H. Erickson.* New York: Irvington Publishers.

Koestler, A. (1967). *The Ghost in the Machine.* Chicago: Henry Regnery Company.

Olness, K. & Libbey, P. (1987). Unrecognized biologic bases of behavioral symptoms in patients referred for hypnotherapy. *American Journal of Clinical Hypnosis, 30*, 1, 1-8.

Rossi, E. L. (1986). *The Psychobiology of Mind-Body Healing: New Concepts of Therapeutic Hypnosis.* New York: W. W. Norton & Company.